The WIZARD'S LAB
Exhibit guide

All Ages

Skills
Observing, Analyzing, Finding Patterns

Concepts
Swing Rate of a Pendulum, Resonance, Oscillating Motion, Superposition of Motion, Speed of Rotation, Angular Momentum, Magnetism, Magnetic Poles, Electricity, Batteries, Generators, Electrodes, Electrolytes, Solar Energy, Solar Cells, Series and Parallel Circuits, Light, Lens Focal Length, Focal Point, Lens Curvature, Images, Light, Polarization of Light, Color, Sound, Superposition of Waves, Amplitude, Wavelength

Themes
Systems & Interactions, Models & Simulations, Patterns of Change, Stability, Scale, Energy, Matter

Nature of Science and Mathematics
Interdisciplinary, Creativity & Constraints, Theory-Based and Testable, Real-Life Applications, Science and Technology

Cary Sneider
Alan Gould

WHAT ARE THEMES?
Themes can be seen as major, recurring ideas that provide a framework for the science curriculum. For more on what GEMS means by themes, please see page... v

Great Explorations in Math and Science (GEMS)
Lawrence Hall of Science
University of California at Berkeley
Berkeley, CA 94720

Illustrations
Carol Bevilacqua
Lisa Klofkorn

Photographs
Richard Hoyt
Cary Sneider

Lawrence Hall of Science, University of California, Berkeley, CA 94720.
Chairman: Glenn T. Seaborg; Director: Marian C. Diamond

Initial support for the origination and publication of the GEMS series was provided by the A.W. Mellon Foundation and the Carnegie Corporation of New York. GEMS has also received support from the McDonnell Douglas Foundation and the McDonnell Douglas Employees Community Fund, the Hewlett Packard Company Foundation, and the people at Chevron USA. GEMS also gratefully acknowledges the contribution of word processing equipment from Apple Computer, Inc. This support does not imply responsibility for statements or views expressed in publications of the GEMS program. Under a grant from the National Science Foundation, GEMS Leader's Workshops have been held across the country. For further information on GEMS leadership opportunities, or to receive a publication brochure and the *GEMS Network News*, please contact GEMS at the address and phone number below.

©1989 by The Regents of The University of California. All rights reserved. Printed in the United States of America. Reprinted with revisions, 1992, 1996.

International Standard Book Number: 0-912511-71-0

COMMENTS WELCOME

Great Explorations in Math and Science (GEMS) is an ongoing curriculum development project. GEMS guides are revised periodically, to incorporate teacher comments and new approaches. We welcome your criticisms, suggestions, helpful hints, and any anecdotes about your experience presenting GEMS activities. Your suggestions will be reviewed each time a GEMS guide is revised. Please send your comments to: GEMS Revisions, c/o Lawrence Hall of Science, University of California, Berkeley, CA 94720.
The phone number is (510) 642-7771.

Great Explorations in Math and Science (GEMS) Program

The Lawrence Hall of Science (LHS) is a public science center on the University of California at Berkeley campus. LHS offers a full program of activities for the public, including workshops and classes, exhibits, films, lectures, and special events. LHS is also a center for teacher education and curriculum research and development.

Over the years, LHS staff have developed a multitude of activities, assembly programs, classes, and interactive exhibits. These programs have proven to be successful at the Hall and should be useful to schools, other science centers, museums, and community groups. A number of these guided-discovery activities have been published under the Great Explorations in Math and Science (GEMS) title, after an extensive refinement process that includes classroom testing of trial versions, modifications to ensure the use of easy-to-obtain materials, and carefully written and edited step-by-step instructions and background information to allow presentation by teachers without special background in mathematics or science.

Staff

Glenn T. Seaborg, *Principal Investigator*
Jacqueline Barber, *Director*
Cary Sneider, *Curriculum Specialist*
Katharine Barrett, Edna DeVore, John Erickson, Jaine Kopp, Kimi Hosoume, Laura Lowell, Linda Lipner, Laura Tucker, Carolyn Willard, *Staff Development Specialists*
Jan M. Goodman, *Mathematics Consultant*
Cynthia Ashley, *Administrative Coordinator*
Gabriela Solomon, *Distribution Coordinator*
Lisa Haderlie Baker, *Art Director*
Carol Bevilacqua and Lisa Klofkorn, *Designers*
Lincoln Bergman and Kay Fairwell, *Editors*

Contributing Authors

Jacqueline Barber
Katharine Barrett
Lincoln Bergman
Jaine Kopp
Linda Lipner
Laura Lowell
Linda De Lucchi
Jean Echols
Jan M. Goodman
Alan Gould
Kimi Hosoume
Sue Jagoda
Larry Malone
Cary I. Sneider
Jennifer Meux White
Carolyn Willard

Reviewers

We would like to thank the following educators who reviewed, tested, or coordinated the reviewing of this series of GEMS materials in manuscript form. Their critical comments and recommendations contributed significantly to these GEMS publications. Their participation does not necessarily imply endorsement of the GEMS program.

FINLAND
Sture Björk
Abo Akademi, Vasa
Mätti Erätuuli
University of Helsinki

KENTUCKY
Amy S. Lowen
Theresa H. Mattei
Mike Plamp
Dr. William M. Sudduth
Museum of History and Science, Louisville
Ken Rosenbaum
Jefferson County Public Schools, Louisville

NEW YORK
Sigrin Newell
Discovery Center, Albany

NORTH CAROLINA
Jorge Escobar
James D. Keighton
Paul Nicholson
North Carolina Museum of Life and Science, Durham
Ed Gray
Sue Griswold
Mike Jordan
John Paschal
Cathy Preiss
Carol Sawyer
Patricia J. Wainland
Discovery Place, Charlotte

OREGON
Shab Levy
Oregon Museum of Science and Industry

WASHINGTON
David Foss
Stuart Kendall
Dennis Schatz
William C. Schmitt
David Taylor
Pacific Science Center, Seattle

Special Note to the Second Edition

This second edition of the *Wizard's Lab*, which documents ten interactive exhibits developed at the Lawrence Hall of Science, is being published in a booklet format, rather than the folder and separate exhibit packets of the first edition. Other than this format change, the content of the ten exhibits remains the same. For this edition we have added some literature connections, and noted the major science themes that these exhibits feature. For more on what GEMS means by "themes," see page *v* of this book.

Since the original publication of the *Wizard's Lab*, the GEMS project has grown in many ways. Meanwhile, the "Wizard's Lab" discovery room for the public at the Lawrence Hall of Science has remained a highly popular place for young and old alike. This special note suggests a new way for you to bring this excitement into your classroom.

In the Introductory section, we mention the possibility of using these exhibits in a school rather than a science center setting, for example, in a school "discovery room." Another way you could do this is to set them up as "learning stations" in the classroom.

Classroom Learning Stations

A learning station is a classroom table, cluster of desks, or counter-top, set up with equipment or materials designed to encourage students to make their own discoveries. The GEMS guide *Bubble Festival* provides detail on ways to set up classroom learning stations featuring bubble activities.

Depending on your time constraints and class needs, you could set up one *Wizard's Lab* exhibit learning station, with the necessary equipment and cartoon signs, somewhere in the room, where small groups of students could experiment at different times. Or you could set up several of these exhibits in different parts of the classroom and have the whole class take part, with groups rotating from one table to the next. Or you could organize a "Wizard's Lab Festival" using most or all of the exhibits for a family night or other school or community gathering.

Many of these exhibits are relatively easy to set up and use accessible materials; you could enlist the help of students in obtaining materials and setting up the learning stations. Others require special equipment that may be available from high school physics labs. **Even if you have only the time and resources to set up just a few of the exhibits as learning stations, it will be of great educational benefit.**

Increasingly, teachers around the country have been using learning stations as a way to enrich classroom experience, enabling discovery learning and free exploration. We would appreciate hearing the ways you combine these table-top exhibits with classroom activities, and any other ideas and suggestions you may have. Thanks for your interest in GEMS!

MORE ON THEMES

The word "themes" is used in many different ways in both ordinary usage and in educational circles. In the GEMS series, themes are seen as key recurring ideas that cut across all the scientific disciplines. Themes are bigger than facts, concepts, or theories. They link various theories from many disciplines. They have also been described as "the sap that runs through the curriculum," to convey the sense that they permeate through and arise from the curriculum. By listing the themes that run through a particular GEMS unit on the title page, we hope to assist you in seeing where the unit fits into the "big picture" of science, and how the unit connects to other GEMS units. The theme "Patterns of Change," for example, suggests that the unit or some important part of it exemplifies larger scientific ideas about why, how, and in what ways change takes place, whether it be a chemical reaction or a caterpillar becoming a butterfly. GEMS has selected 10 major themes:

Systems & Interactions	**Scale**
Models & Simulations	**Structure**
Stability	**Energy**
Patterns of Change	**Matter**
Evolution	**Diversity & Unity**

If you are interested in thinking more about themes and the thematic approach to teaching and constructing curriculum, you may wish to obtain a copy of our handbook, *To Build A House: GEMS and the Thematic Approach to Teaching Science*. For more information and an order brochure, write or call GEMS, Lawrence Hall of Science, University of California, Berkeley, CA 94720. (510) 642-7771. **Thanks for your interest in GEMS!**

CONTENTS

Overview vii
Resonant Pendula 1
Harmonograph 9
Spinning Platform 19
Floating Disks 29
Electricity Makers 37
Human Battery 47
Solar Cells 55
Lenses 67
Polarizers 79
Sounds 87
Literature Connections 99

EXHIBIT ▲ GUIDE

OVERVIEW
THE WIZARD'S LAB
A Science Discovery Room for People of All Ages

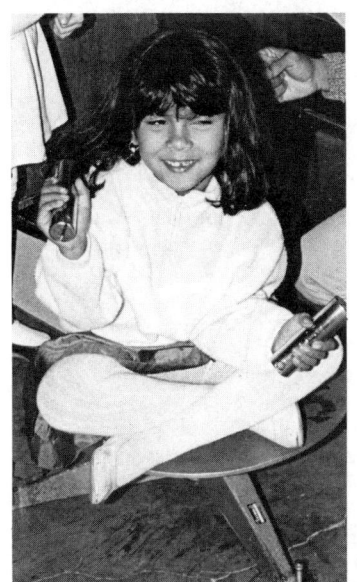
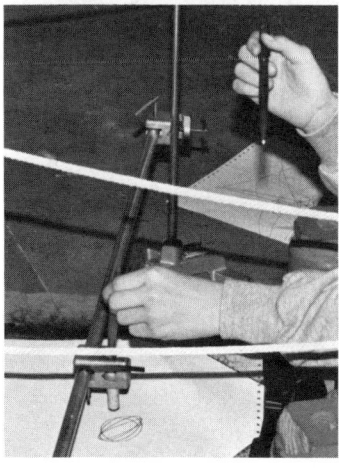
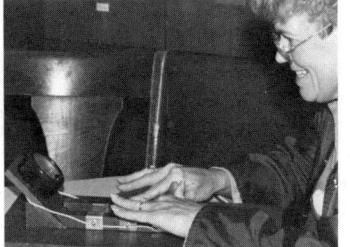

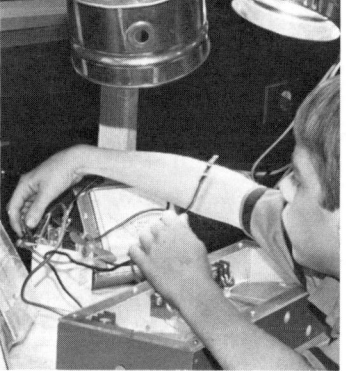
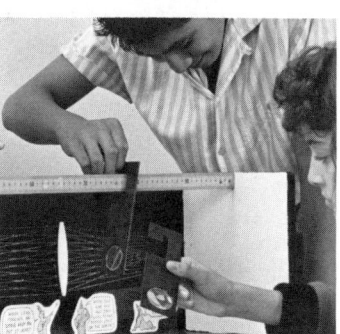

A Series of Interactive Exhibits Including...

- ▶ **Resonant Pendula**
- ▶ **Harmonograph**
- ▶ **Spinning Platform**
- ▶ **Floating Disks**
- ▶ **Electricity Makers**
- ▶ **Human Battery**
- ▶ Solar Cells
- ▶ Lenses
- ▶ Polarizers
- ▶ Sounds

OVERVIEW

Acknowledgments

The Wizard's Lab was created by Budd Wentz in 1976 at the Lawrence Hall of Science. Tom Latimer, a cartoonist and science teacher, created the Wizard cartoon character, along with many of the cartoon instructions still used today. Since the Wizard's Lab began, many volunteers and staff members have contributed ideas and created new exhibits. Those who have made major contributions include: Alan Friedman, Mark Gingrich, Tony Bond, Charles Yum, John Erickson, George Corrigan, and Alan Gould. Finnish educator Matti Eratuuli conducted a thorough evaluation of the Wizard's Lab in 1987, offered many suggestions for improving the exhibits, and assisted in preparing this Exhibit Guide. ▲

Exhibit Descriptions

The Resonant Pendula exhibit is a loosely-supported rod with several pendula hanging from it. Visitors swing one pendulum and are surprised to discover that as the pendulum slows down, a different pendulum that is the same length starts swinging.

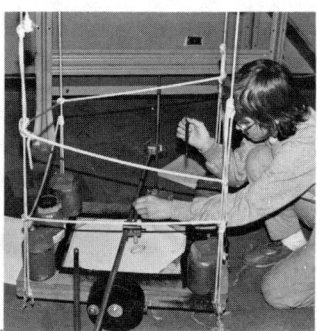

The Harmonograph exhibit involves visitors in making intricate geometric patterns by positioning a pen in the center of a large sheet of paper on a heavy platform. The pen traces overlapping circular shapes as the platform swings back and forth and side to side. The exhibit illustrates how periodic motion changes slowly and regularly.

The Spinning Platform exhibit is a turntable on which the visitor sits and holds two weights. With an initial push by another visitor, the person on the turntable can alter the rate of spin by holding the weights at different distances from her body.

The Floating Disks exhibit is a series of ring-shaped magnets on a rod, arranged so similar poles face each other. The visitor is challenged to figure out why they "float," and to build a similar stack of magnets.

The Electricity Makers exhibit invites people to make the needle of an ammeter move by connecting it with two wires to wet cells or dynamos. By manipulating the equipment, visitors discover how to produce stronger or weaker currents.

The Human Battery exhibit demonstrates a way to make electricity chemically. By touching two electrodes the visitor's body serves as the electrolyte, and the resulting voltage causes a needle on the voltmeter to move. Touching different pairs of electrodes made of different metals produces more or less electricity.

The Solar Cells exhibit allows visitors to connect solar cells in series or parallel to a voltmeter and ammeter, or to an electric motor with a propeller. The visitors control the amount of electricity produced by connecting the cells in different ways, or by blocking light from a lamp.

The Lenses exhibit provides opportunities to manipulate three different lenses — individually or together — to discover how to make upside-down and right-side-up images, and images of different sizes.

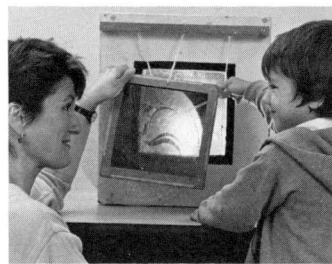

The Polarizers exhibit is a pair of polaroid filters with various pieces of clear plastic in between them. By manipulating these materials in front of a light source visitors see beautiful colored patterns.

The Sounds exhibit provides an opportunity for visitors to see a graphic display of sound waves. In one oscilloscope exhibit, the visitors "see" the sound of their own voice. In a second oscilloscope exhibit they see beautiful geometric patterns on the screen that are very similar to the paper patterns created by the *Harmonograph* exhibit. ▲

Introduction

The Wizard's Lab is a physics discovery room at the Lawrence Hall of Science in Berkeley, California. Visitors interact with the exhibits by manipulating objects, turning switches, spinning wheels, observing surprising phenomena, performing experiments, and, in some cases, becoming part of the exhibits themselves. The

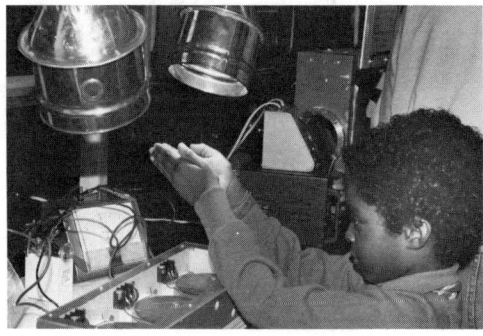

opportunity to enjoy doing experiments is the main ingredient for success. Even people who claim to "hate science" learn some scientific principles while having a good time in the Wizard's Lab.

This Exhibit Guide folder is designed to help you create a Wizard's Lab at your school, science center, scout troop meeting place, summer camp, or other appropriate location. Each of the exhibit descriptions

O V E R V I E W

in this Exhibit Guide provides information on creating one complete Wizard's Lab exhibit, from acquiring the materials to construction and signage. This Overview also provides suggestions for inventing your own exhibits.

If you do not have an entire room to devote to a Wizard's Lab, or the time to assemble a lot of equipment, you can begin with just one or two exhibits. One way to get started is to set up a Wizard's Lab in connection with some special event such as a science fair, school celebration, or careers day. Building the exhibits so they can be stored in a safe place will allow you to set them up easily at the next opportunity. Eventually, you can expand the collection until it becomes an entire room of exciting things to do. ▲

Why a "Wizard?"

When we first created this science discovery room we tried out different names. Some people were reluctant to even enter "The Physics Lab" because of their previous experience with high school physics. Themes like "The Physics Fun Room" were somewhat better, but did not have the visitor appeal of "The Wizard's Lab."

The word "wizard" has some non-scientific connotations. The first uses of the word in 15th century

England referred to people skilled in astrology and alchemy. In fact, many of the great scientists of the Renaissance were also astrologers and alchemists. However, the broadest definition of "wizard" is a philosopher, sage, wise person, or one who does "wonders" in a particular field or profession. The scientific explanations provided for the phenomena explored in the Wizard's Lab clearly demonstrate to visitors that the exhibits are about science, not magic or sorcery.

Whether or not you decide to use the name "Wizard's Lab," or to include the particular exhibits described in this folder, your discovery room is most likely to be an exciting and educational place for visitors if it incorporates the following qualities:

▶ Each Wizard's Lab exhibit requires the visitor to do something and think about it — not just look or push a button. Visitors need to manipulate equipment, observe phenomena, answer a question, and become actively involved in the exhibits.

▶ The Wizard cartoon characters are a unique feature of the Wizard's Lab. Years of experience have shown that visitors to the Wizard's Lab

OVERVIEW

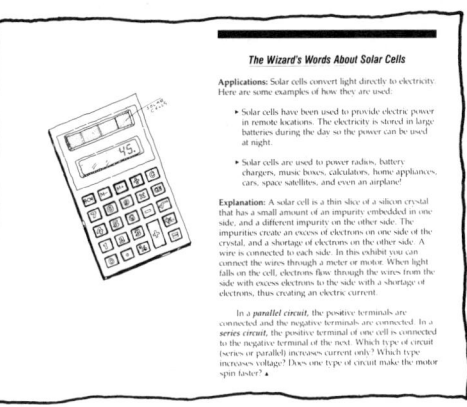

read cartoon instructions — even people who would refuse to read a sign with the same words printed in large type. There's something compelling about cartoon characters that intrigues just about any visitor.

▶ Visitors who are curious to learn more can ask the person in charge of the lab, or turn the cartoon sign around for further activities, examples of the phenomenon in real life, and a brief explanation of the scientific principle behind the exhibit.

A research study of Wizard's Lab visitors has shown that a discovery room with these qualities provides visitors with an enjoyable experience and that visitors are also very successful in observing phenomena and understanding scientific principles.

Construction Materials and Signs

In selecting exhibits to document, we chose those that can be made with materials available from most hardware, electronics, or variety stores, and lumberyards. If you're a "scrounger," and have access to lumber scraps or companies that toss out interesting waste, many of these exhibits can be built for very little money. In fact, only a couple of the exhibits described in this folder require more expensive equipment, and you may choose not to include these in your Wizard's Lab.

Each of the exhibit descriptions in this folder includes a Wizard cartoon and an explanation sheet called "The Wizard's Words," both of which can be duplicated. Hand-coloring the cartoons can make them more attractive. These signs can be mounted in a variety of ways. One way is to mount the Wizard cartoon on a sheet of cardboard, and then tape the cardboard to a larger sheet of cardboard along one edge to make a hinge. Mount the explanation sheet underneath the cartoon so visitors can lift the cartoon to read "The Wizard's Words." A tab at the bottom or side of the cartoon should be labeled "Lift for More Information!" The sign can then be taped to a table or wall near the exhibit.

A second method for mounting the cartoon and explanation sheets is to tape them to opposite sides of a stand so the visitor can turn the stand around to read either the cartoon or the explanation. One way of making a stand is to cut a 12" x 24" rectangle of sheet aluminum and bend it in the middle to form an A-frame. Sand the corners. Insert the cartoon and explanation sheets in plastic sheet protectors and tape these onto opposite sides of the A-frame with 2" wide transparent tape. Place a label at the top or bottom of the cartoon saying "Turn around for more information!" Place the stand so visitors can see the cartoon when approaching the exhibit.

O V E R V I E W

Inventing New Exhibits

You can also invent your own Wizard's Lab exhibits. One source of ideas and equipment is a high school or college science lab. Most labs have a storage room with equipment that is used for demonstrations only once or twice a year. If you do invent new exhibits, keep in mind the need to visitor-proof them by increasing their sturdiness and eliminating safety hazards. For example, fragile items can be enclosed in boxes with clear plastic windows and manipulated from the outside with knobs or levers. Most ideas for visitor-proofing will result from fixing the exhibits. After the second or third repair you will undoubtedly think of ways to keep visitors from damaging an exhibit in precisely that way again!

If you decide to invent new exhibits you will need to create your own Wizard cartoons and "The Wizard's Words" explanation sheets. The cartoons should be designed to get the visitors started by suggesting what they should do or by asking a question they can answer by experimenting. Sketch the exhibit, and trace one or two wizards in the appropriate spots. Draw a speaking bubble so the wizard appears to be telling the visitor what to do while pointing at or sitting on the part of the exhibit that should be manipulated. Wizards and speaking bubbles can also be attached directly to the exhibit itself, showing the visitors what to do or observe. Make extra copies of the cartoons and explanation sheets so you can later replace signs that become worn or lost.

Demonstrations

A five-to ten-minute demonstration once every half-hour is a popular addition to a day in the Wizard's Lab. The demonstration can focus on some of the exhibits or on other equipment that is too complicated, or too dangerous, to allow visitors to interact with on their own. Our Wizard's Lab at Lawrence Hall of Science includes an electricity demonstration of a Jacob's Ladder, Tesla Coil, and Van de Graaff Generator. (These devices are described in *The Magic of Electricity*, a GEMS school Assembly Presenter's Guide.) Other demonstrations could explore laser light, vacuum pumps, or liquid nitrogen and dry ice.

Setting Up the Room

Organize the exhibits by themes. You might put up large signs so the visitors can identify the theme areas, such as "electricity," "light," or "magnetism." If you have demonstrations, place the equipment that you plan to use in the front, or to one side of the room. If your demonstration uses dangerous equipment, rope off the part of the room where that equipment is kept, and unplug or otherwise disable the apparatus so visitors are not tempted to try it by themselves!

Wizards Training

It will be of great benefit to your visitors if they have a guide in the room who shares some of the most important characteristics of the cartoon wizard. This wizard-guide is a teacher who helps visitors see the phenomenon for themselves, rather than describing it for them. The wizard-guide suggests what to do at each exhibit, but will only explain the scientific principle after the visitor has done the experiment. The guide helps people make discoveries at their own pace, and in response to their own interests.

Hold a training session for the staff or volunteers who will serve as "wizards." Naturally, you'll want to discuss the ways of setting up and maintaining the equipment. However, discussing effective ways of interacting with the public is just as important. Demonstrate to the volunteers how you would like them to show visitors what they can do with the exhibits if they seem puzzled. Emphasize that the task of a "wizard" is to help people make their own discoveries—it is not to do the experiment for the visitor or to offer lengthy explanations. So visitors know who to go to for help, the "wizard" should wear some identification, such as a badge, brightly-colored jacket, or special T-shirt.

What should the "wizard" do when an exhibit breaks down? Broken exhibits can be frustrating for visitors, especially when they may not be aware that the exhibit is broken. Often they assume it is their fault that it won't work. Keep a tool kit in the room so the "wizard" on duty can attempt to fix it on the spot. When that's impossible, the broken exhibit should be removed from the room, or labeled with an "Out of Order" sign.

Final Thoughts

Now that the Wizard's Lab at Lawrence Hall of Science is over ten years old, we've learned that only one thing is constant — change! New volunteers have uncontrollable urges to build new exhibits. Older exhibits sometimes defy visitor-proofing and occasionally break down along with our patience. A new item in the science gift shop is so exciting that it must be made into an exhibit, complete with cartoon instructions. The Wizard's Lab takes on a life of its own. It is far more than a collection of classic science exhibits and people to watch over them. It is a dynamic entity, attracting childen, adults, families, professional scientists, and even people who didn't realize they were interested in science. For many, it's a great way to spend an afternoon. For others, it provides inspiration for a school science project, a way to appreciate what scientists do, or maybe even a glimmer of a career in science or engineering. ▲

by
Cary Sneider and Alan Gould

EXHIBIT GUIDE

Resonant PENDULA

THE WIZARD'S LAB

RESONANT PENDULA

Skills
Observing, Analyzing, Finding Patterns

Concepts
Swing Rate of a Pendulum, Resonance

Themes
Patterns of Change, Stability, Scale, Energy,
Systems & Interactions, Models & Simulations

INTRODUCTION

*I*n this exhibit, visitors are invited to swing one of several pendula attached to a bar, and to observe what happens to the other pendula. Surprisingly, only one of the other pendula starts and keeps on swinging, and that pendulum has the same length as the first pendulum. This phenomenon is called *resonance*—the two pendula affect each other's movements because they have the same length and therefore the same rate of swing. Thus, they *resonate* with each other.

How does swinging one pendulum affect the other pendula attached to the bar? By observing the apparatus closely, visitors may notice that swinging the first pendulum causes the supporting bar to twist a little. Longer and shorter pendula are pushed by the bar, but they do not swing very much. They do not resonate with the first pendulum because they have different lengths and therefore different rates of swing. Some visitors experiment further by swinging a pendulum in circles or ovals to see if that also starts the resonant pendulum swinging.

Visitors who wish to read "The Wizard's Words" about this exhibit find that other examples of this phenomenon include pushing a child on a swing, mounting car engines, and designing bridges. ▲

MATERIALS

- 1 sheet of wood (¾" x 12" x 30") for a baseboard
- 3 wood dowels (¾" diameter, 24" long) for poles and pivot bar
- 5 wood dowels (¼" diameter, with lengths: 5", 5", 9", 15", 15")
- 2 wood blocks (1½" x 3½" x 3½") for pole supports
- 7 hooks (½" diameter)
- 5 screw eyes (½" diameter)
- 2 nails (8D common)
- 10 washers for use as weights (¾" diameter)
- screws, nails, and glue as needed

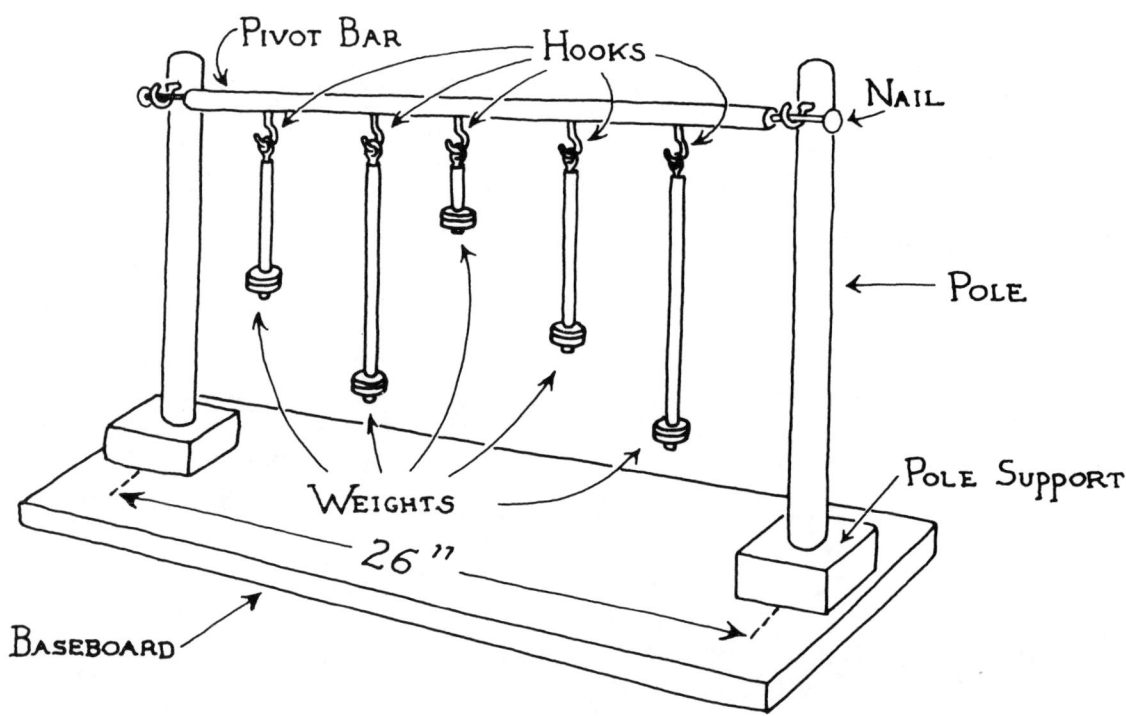

EXHIBIT
CONSTRUCTION

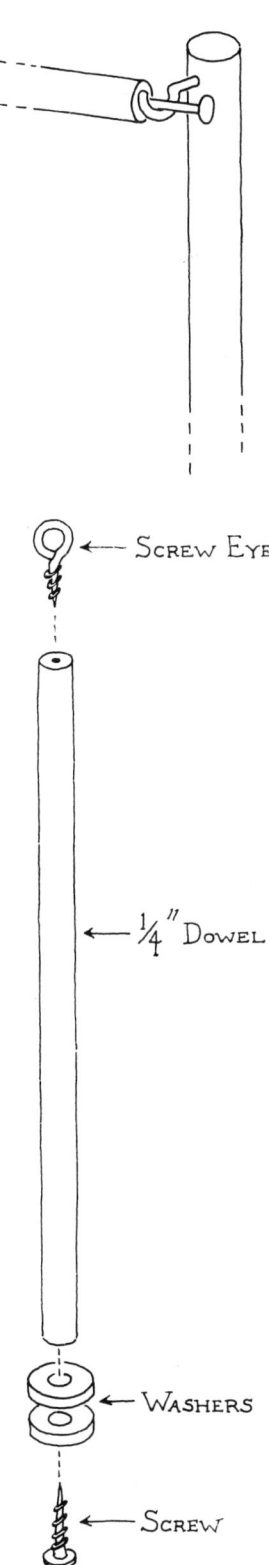

1. Drill a ¾" hole in the center of each block to serve as pole supports.

2. Secure the pole supports to the ends of the baseboard using nails (or screws) and glue so their holes are 26" apart.

3. Glue a ¾" dowel into each pole support. For easier storage, don't glue.

4. Use the third ¾" dowel for the pivot bar. Into each end of the pivot bar drill a hole lengthwise, with a diameter such that the 8D nail will force fit into it.

5. Force a nail into each end hole in the pivot bar. Leave at least 1½" of the nail protruding from the end of the bar.

6. Screw in a hook 1" from the top of each pole and position the pivot bar horizontally between the poles with the nails resting on the hooks.

7. Screw in five hooks evenly spaced and in line with each other, across the length of the pivot bar.

8. Drill a hole lengthwise in the top and bottom ends of each ¼" dowel. Screw a screw eye into one end. Use a screw to attach two washers to the other end.

9. Hook the ¼" dowels to the hooks on the bar. Adjust the lengths of the pendula if necessary by turning the screw eyes so there are two long pendula of equal length, two short pendula of equal length, and one pendulum whose length is in between. "Equal lengths" should be as equal as possible.

10. Paint with latex enamel, varnish, or stain all wooden parts. ▲

The Wizard's RESONANT PENDULA

Start ONE weight swinging. Watch to see which other weight starts swinging the most.

Do pendula of the SAME length or DIFFERENT lengths swing together?

The Wizard's Words About Resonant Pendula

Applications: When you start one pendulum swinging, another pendulum of the same length starts swinging too, because it swings at the same rate. This is one example of *resonance*. Other examples include:

▶ When pushing a person on a swing, you time the pushes at the same rate as the swing goes back and forth so each push gets the child to swing higher and higher.

▶ Car engine mounts are designed so they do not vibrate at the same rate as the engine. Otherwise, the vibrations will get bigger and bigger until the engine breaks loose.

▶ The Tacoma Narrows Bridge was entirely destroyed because it vibrated at the same rate as gusts of wind.

Explanation: In this exhibit, when you start one pendulum swinging it twists the bar a little on each swing. This back-and-forth twist gives tiny pushes to each of the other pendula attached to the bar. Watch carefully, and you will see that only one other pendulum keeps increasing its swing, and that pendulum has the same length as the pendulum you first set in motion. This happens because pendula of the same length swing at the same rate. So, the first pendulum gives pushes to the second pendulum at just the right rate to get it swinging higher and higher on each push. When the swing rates or vibrations of two such objects are timed like this, we say they are *in resonance*. ▲

EXHIBIT MAINTENANCE

1. If some visitors remove the pivot bar, you can replace the hooks holding it in place with a closed screw eye that is smaller than the diameter of the nail heads driven into the ends of the pivot bar.

2. Pendula may "disappear." Have spares on hand. ▲

EXHIBIT GUIDE

HARMONOGRAPH

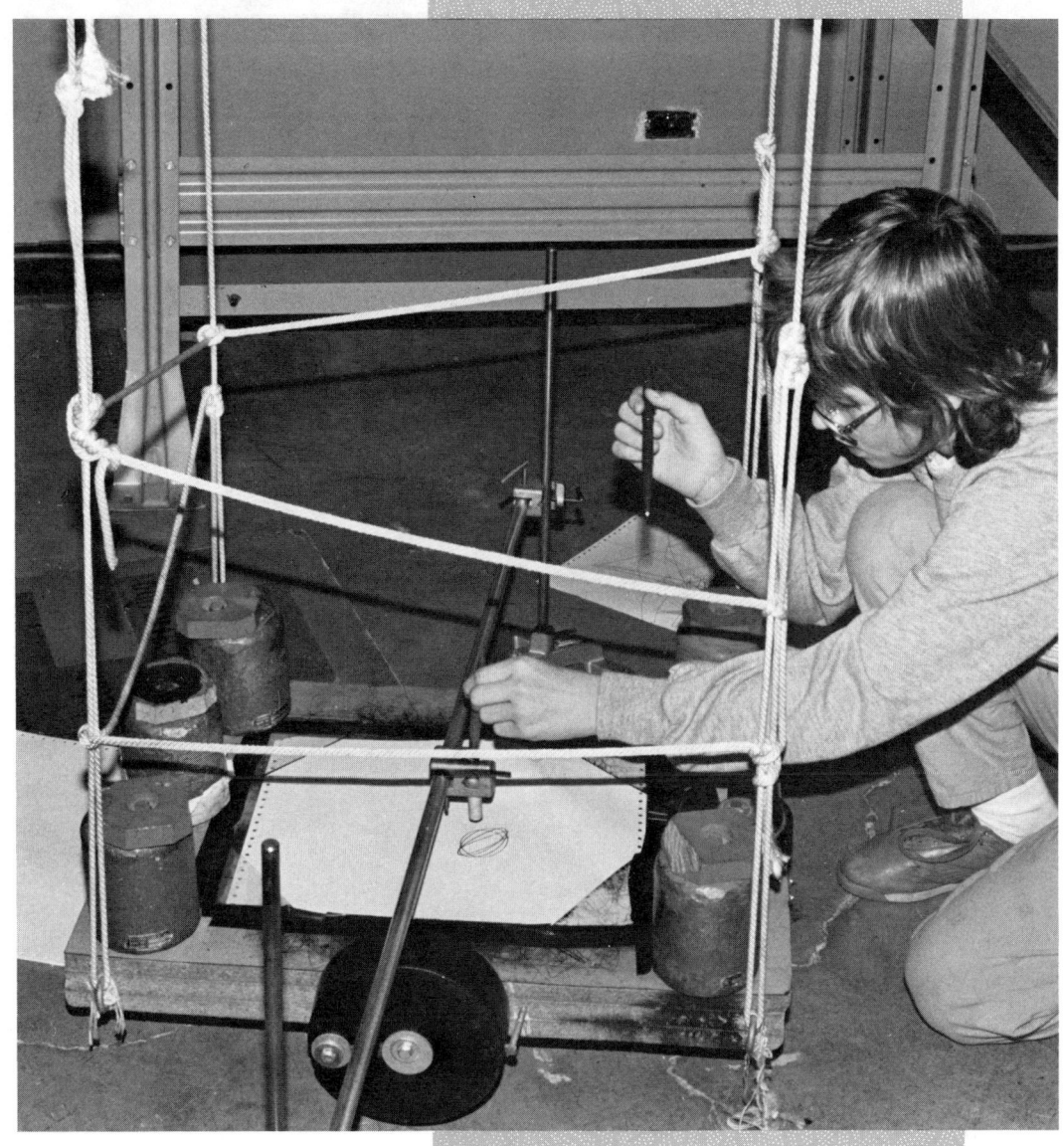

THE WIZARD'S LAB

HARMONOGRAPH

Skills
Observing, Analyzing, Finding Patterns

Concepts
Oscillating Motion, Superposition of Motion

Themes
Patterns of Change, Stability, Scale, Energy,
Systems & Interactions, Models & Simulations

INTRODUCTION

*T*he harmonograph is a heavy platform hung by ropes from four hooks in the ceiling. A stationary pen holder is rigidly fixed above the swinging platform. The visitor places a sheet of paper onto the platform, and puts a felt-tipped pen loosely into the pen holder so the pen's own weight causes it to draw on the paper. The visitor then raises the pen for a moment while she pulls the platform to the side and lets it go. Then she drops the pen and watches the harmonograph draw a beautiful geometric pattern! The secret of a clear, even drawing is to let the harmonograph swing without touching it.

Visitors who wish to learn more about the shapes drawn by the harmonograph can read "The Wizard's Words" about how the different motions combine to create the figures. This is called the principle of *superposition.*

Your harmonograph can be made to fit any size paper that is available. Computer paper that has been printed on one side is economical, ecological, and provides a large picture area. A major attraction of this exhibit is that it provides visitors with a "work of art" to take home. ▲

MATERIALS

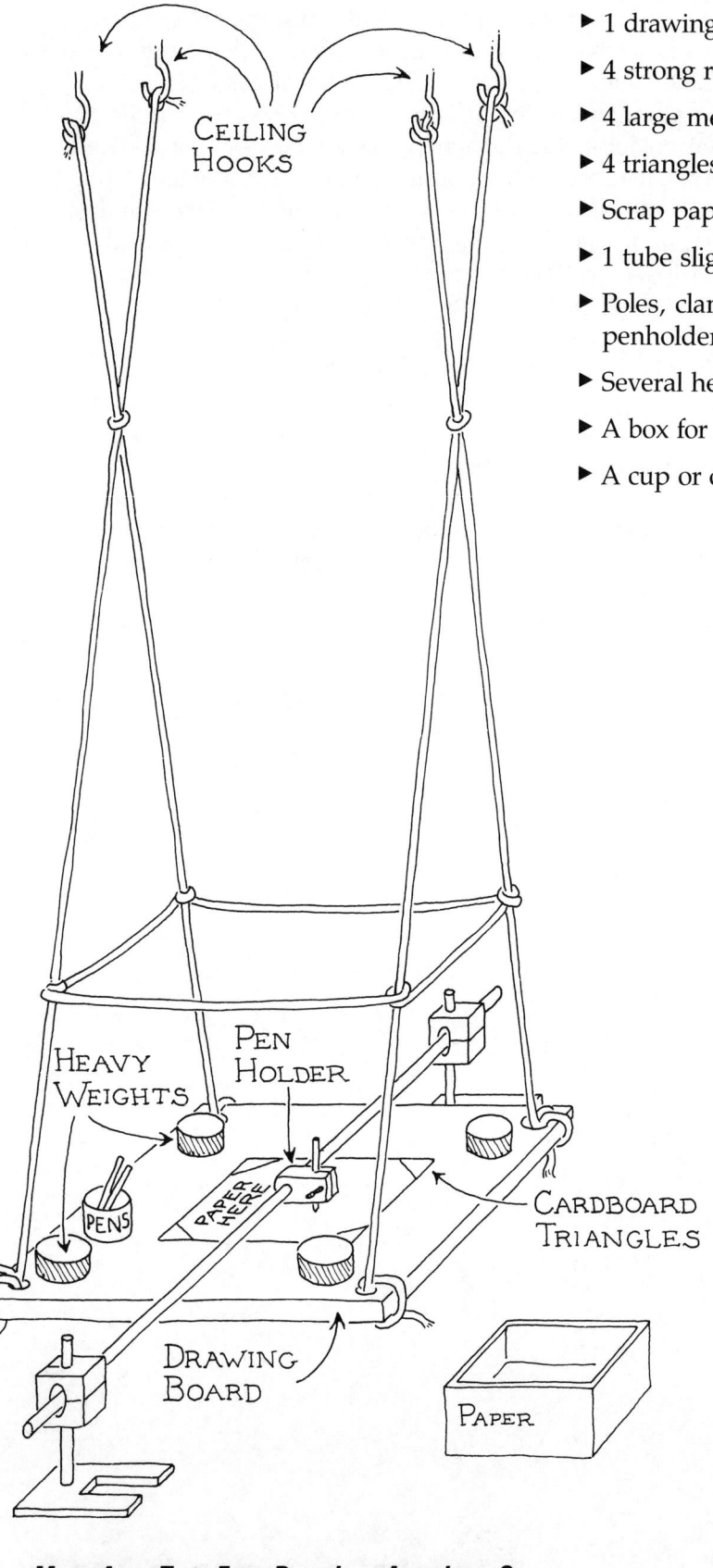

- 1 drawing board (¾" x 24" x 24")
- 4 strong ropes that stretch from ceiling to floor
- 4 large metal wood screw hooks
- 4 triangles of cardboard
- Scrap paper and felt-tipped pens of various colors
- 1 tube slightly larger than the pens for pen holder
- Poles, clamps, and stands, or scrap wood to make penholder support
- Several heavy weights (5–10 kg. each)
- A box for holding paper
- A cup or can for holding pens

EXHIBIT CONSTRUCTION

1. Find two sturdy beams or joists in the ceiling in which to screw the four hooks at the corners of an imaginary rectangle, about 24" x 24".

2. Tie a length of rope from each hook. Tie the ropes together in pairs, about 2 feet from the ceiling, as shown in the diagram.

3. Drill a ½" diameter hole in each corner of the drawing board platform.

4. Loop the bottom end of one of the hanging ropes through each hole and tie a knot that will make adjusting the lengths of the ropes easy. Temporarily adjust the ropes so the drawing board hangs horizontally about one foot above the floor.

5. Place the heavy weights on corners of the drawing board. Leave enough clear space in the middle for the paper to lie flat. Distribute the weights so they balance and the platform remains horizontal. The ropes will stretch considerably. Secure the weights to the drawing board.

6. Readjust the ropes so the drawing board is horizontal, and at least 4 inches above the floor.

7. Tape cardboard triangle pieces to the drawing board as corner holders for the drawing paper. Label the center area of the drawing board "PUT DRAWING PAPER HERE."

CONSTRUCTION

8. Using scrap wood or laboratory poles and clamps, build a mounting for the pen holder tube. The pen holder tube must be held vertically over the drawing board about one inch above the board. The mount must rest on the floor, but its legs must allow the drawing board to swing unobstructed under the pen at least the length of the drawing paper. Label the pen holder tube "PEN HOLDER."

9. Mount a cup or can on the drawing tray to hold pens of different colors.

10. Place a box of drawing paper nearby and label the box "DRAWING PAPER." ▲

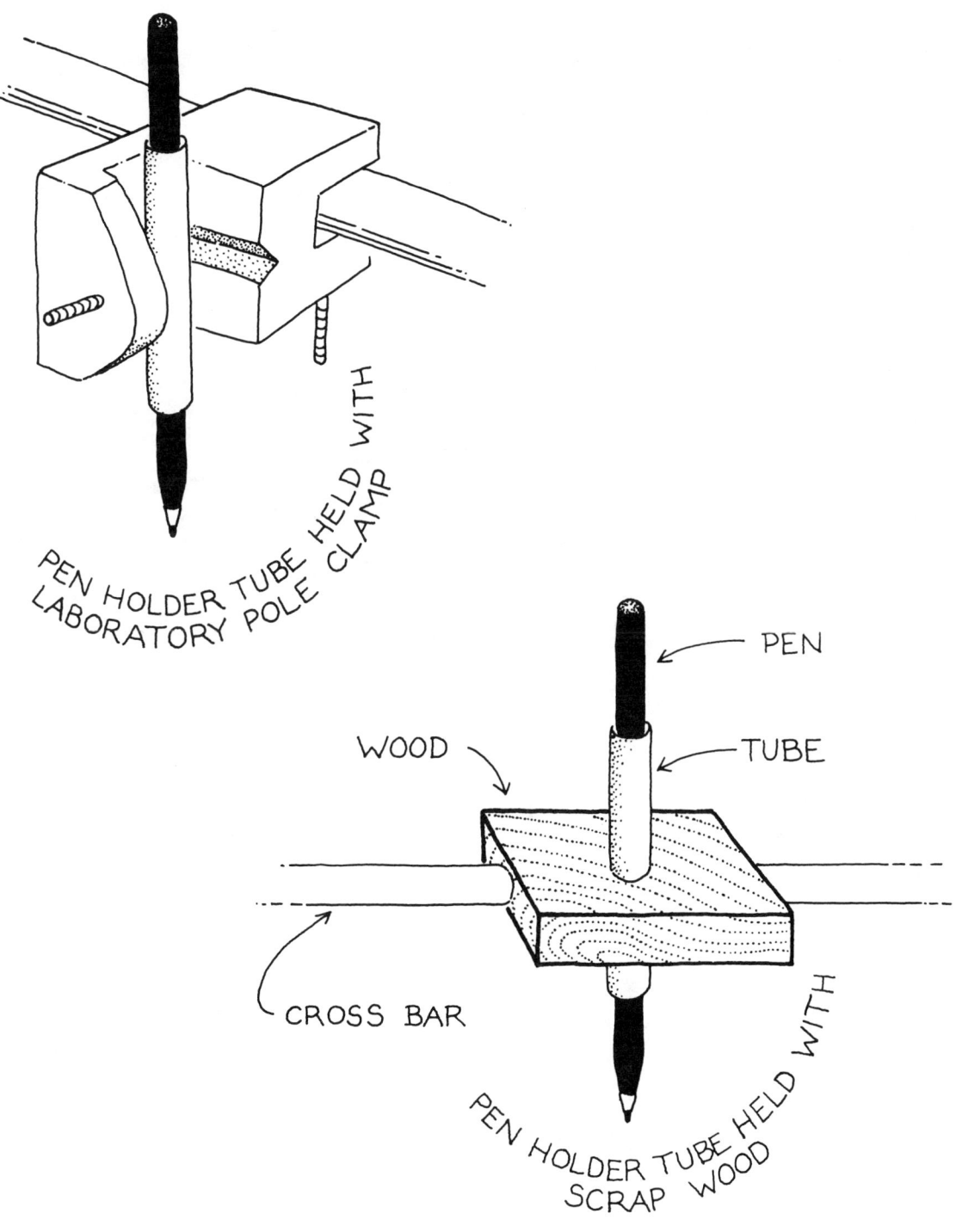

The Wizard's HARMONOGRAPH

Then put the pen in here.

First start the drawing board swinging.

The secret is to let it swing on its own once it has started.

HEY, this is a really swinging place!

The Wizard's Words About Harmonograph

Applications: The harmonograph is a platform that swings from the ceiling. You create a beautiful geometric pattern by placing a piece of paper on the platform and drawing a picture with a pen that stays still while the platform swings under it. Examples of these beautiful shapes include the following:

▶ You can make a sand pendulum by tying a cone-shaped cup to the end of a string, and filling it with sand. Snip the end of the cone so the sand flows out, and start it swinging. As the sand runs out of the hole it will form a beautiful pattern, like your harmonograph picture.

▶ Many science fiction films show television screens (oscilloscopes) with moving patterns of light that form ever-changing circles and ovals. This is an electronic version of the harmonograph.

Explanation: The harmonograph is a swinging *pendulum* made in the shape of a platform. If the platform swings only back and forth, the pen would trace over the same line. However, the platform also swings from side to side. This combination of motions causes the pen to draw a circular or oval shape, called a *Lissajous figure*. Two other factors also affect the shape: the platform twists, making the shape even more complex; and as the platform slows down from friction, the picture area gets smaller. The principle that several different motions add together is called *superposition*. ▲

EXHIBIT MAINTENANCE

1. The ropes stretch and lengthen over time, so they need periodic adjustment to keep the clearance between the drawing board and the pen holder about 1".

2. A supply of paper and pens should be maintained.

3. Put a sign on the drawing tray saying "PLEASE DO NOT STEP HERE!" For further protection string a "fence" from rope to rope around the drawing tray.

4. Another sign might go on the can of pens saying "PLEASE PUT CAPS ON PENS WHEN YOU'RE DONE AND RETURN THEM HERE."

5. Keep a wastebasket nearby with a sign saying "PLEASE DISCARD UNWANTED DRAWINGS HERE." ▲

EXHIBIT ▲ GUIDE

Spinning PLATFORM

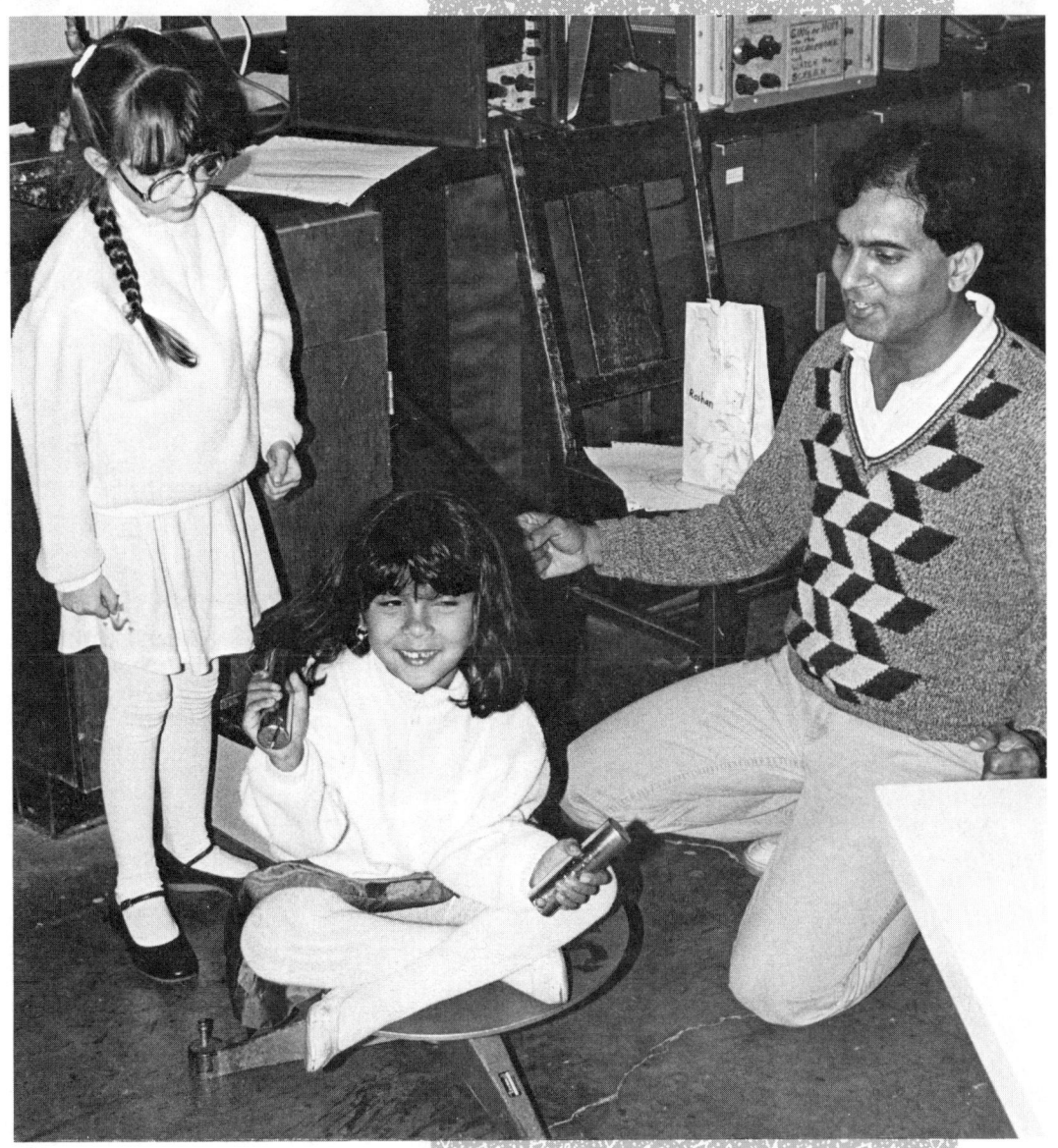

THE WIZARD'S LAB

▶SPINNING PLATFORM

Skills
Observing, Analyzing, Finding Patterns

Concepts
Speed of Rotation, Angular Momentum

Themes
Energy, Scale, Patterns of Change, Stability,
Systems & Interactions, Models & Simulations

INTRODUCTION

*T*he Spinning Platform consists of a sturdy platform mounted on ball bearings so it spins easily. One visitor sits on the platform, holding a weight in each hand. A second visitor starts him spinning. As the seated visitor pulls the weights in toward his chest, the rate of spin increases. Pushing the weights further from his body slows the rate of spin. The fun of spinning leads to an understanding that the rate of spin will increase when the weights are pulled closer to the axis of rotation.

The seated visitor can also start himself spinning by holding a bicycle wheel axle, asking another person to get the wheel spinning, and then changing the orientation of the wheel as he holds it. Visitors interested in how scientists interpret these surprising phenomena can read "The Wizard's Words" about *conservation of angular momentum.* ▲

MATERIALS

- 1 spinning platform (can be made from a 12" diameter lazy susan bearing, an 18" disk of ¾" plywood, and a rubber pad)
- 2 weights—½ kg.
- 2 weights—1 kg.
- 2 weights—5 kg.
- 1 box to hold the weights
- 1 small bicycle wheel
- 1 large bicycle wheel
- 4 aluminum rods, 1" diameter, 3" long

EXHIBIT
CONSTRUCTION

1. If you have a rotating platform from a physics lab, no construction is necessary. If not, you can build one. One way to do this is to purchase a large heavy-duty lazy susan bearing. (e.g., the Triangle model 6C ball bearing assembly is 12" in diameter, rated at 1,000 pounds, and costs under $10). The bearing can be screwed to an 18" diameter wood disk as shown in the diagram, to make a smoothly rotating platform. A rubber pad glued to the bottom of the bearing will prevent slipping.

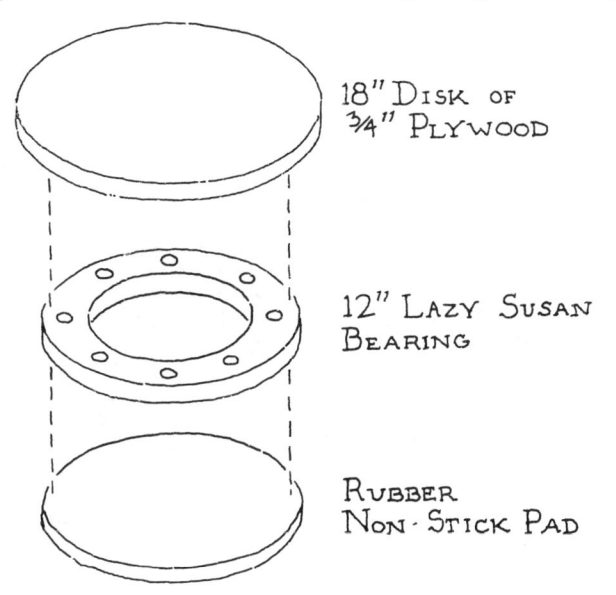

18" Disk of ¾" Plywood

12" Lazy Susan Bearing

Rubber Non-Stick Pad

2. Attach handles to the axle of the bicycle wheel so it is easy to hold while it's spinning. Handles can be made from aluminum rods, drilled and tapped so they screw onto the bolts that extend on either side of the axle. It is good to have one small bicycle wheel and one large one to accommodate people of different sizes. Placing extra weights around the rim, or inserting an inner tube and filling it with water accentuates the desired effect.

3. Cover the spokes of the bicycle wheel with disks of clear flexible plastic (about 1/16" thick) so visitors will not get their fingers stuck in the moving spokes. To fit the plastic, make a cut along the radius of each disk and slide one edge over the other, creating a very shallow cone that conforms to the angle of the spokes. Drill several 1/8" holes in each disk so it can be tied onto the wheel with string or wire.

4. Rope off an area around the exhibit so observers are not hit by the revolving weights. Paint a sign on the platform instructing visitors to "Sit Here—Do Not Stand." ▲

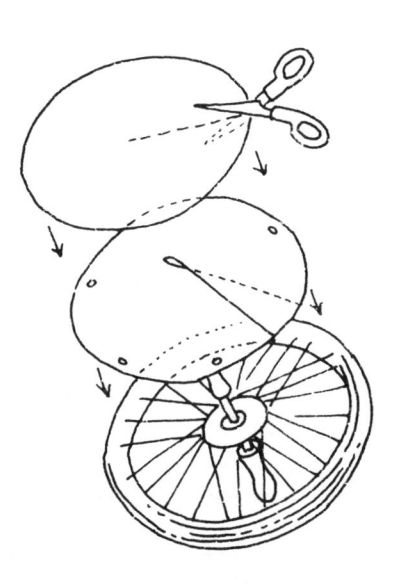

The WIZARD'S SPINNING PLATFORM
HOLDING WEIGHTS

Have a friend start you spinning.

Try putting your arms out straight. Then bend them both inward.

SIT on the platform do NOT stand up!

The Wizard's Words About
Holding Weights on the Spinning Platform

Applications: As you pull the weights toward your chest, you spin faster. Hold them at arms length and you spin slower. This phenomenon is well known by people who play sports. Here are some examples:

▶ As an ice skater brings his arms and legs closer to the center of his body he spins faster and faster and faster!

▶ A gymnast tucks her head and pulls in her legs with her arms so she somersaults faster and faster.

Explanation: A top will keep spinning until friction slows it down. The top's tendency to keep spinning depends on its spin rate, its weight, and its diameter. These three characteristics tell you how hard it is to stop a given top. Their combined effect is the top's *angular momentum*. If one of the three characteristics increases, another characteristic decreases, so the top's **angular momentum always stays the same.**

When you are on the spinning platform, you are just like a top. If you pull the weights inward, your diameter has decreased. You feel your speed increase so your total angular momentum stays the same. If you move the weights further out, the diameter increases, and speed decreases. Again, your total angular momentum still stays the same. ▲

The WIZARD'S SPINNING PLATFORM
HOLDING A BICYCLE WHEEL

Ask a friend to start the wheel spinning.

Tilt the spinning wheel ~ see what happens to you!

SIT on the platform do NOT stand up!

The Wizard's Words about
Holding a Bicycle Wheel on the Spinning Platform

Applications: What happens when you try to tilt the spinning wheel? You probably feel weird forces trying to wrench the bicycle wheel out of your hands and the whole platform turns. Other examples of this phenomenon include the following:

▶ While you are riding a bicycle you have no difficulty keeping your balance. However, when the wheels slow down the bicycle falls over easily.

▶ The earth is a huge spinning sphere. Like the bicycle wheel in this exhibit, the earth tends to keep spinning at the same speed, with its axis pointed in the same direction — toward the North Star.

Explanation: As in the examples above, something that is spinning tends to keep its spin axis pointing the same way. When you try to change the direction of the spin axis of the bicycle wheel, it resists your effort and pushes back. The surprise is that it pushes back in an unexpected direction. If you tilt the handle forward, the force will cause the platform you are sitting on to start rotating. You will find detailed descriptions of this phenomenon and learn how engineers apply it to keeping ships, planes, and spacecraft on course under the heading "Gyroscopes" in most physics textbooks. ▲

EXHIBIT MAINTENANCE

Oil or grease the bearings of the spinning platform periodically. The bearings of the bicycle wheel also need grease once in a while. We have never experienced a problem with the weights being taken, but it's good to have spares on hand. ▲

EXHIBIT GUIDE

FLOATING
DISKS

THE WIZARD'S LAB

FLOATING DISKS

Skills
Observing, Analyzing, Finding Patterns

Concepts
Magnetism, Magnetic Poles

Themes
Energy, Matter, Structure, Stability, Patterns of Change

INTRODUCTION

Visitors who approach this exhibit are amazed to see a series of disks apparently floating in midair! The Wizard's cartoon invites the visitors to pick up other disk-shaped magnets (painted green and red) and place them on an empty stick so they also float. The visitors discover that similar colors, representing similar magnetic poles, must face each other in order for the magnets to float.

Visitors who read "The Wizard's Words" learn a little about the history of the magnetic compass, how magnets are commonly used, different kinds of magnetic materials, the way that atoms are arranged inside magnets, and about how "permanent" magnets can be remagnetized. ▲

MATERIALS

- 6 ring magnets, about 1" diameter, plus several extras
- 2 dowels, 8" long, with a small enough diameter so a ring magnet slides loosely over it
- 2 wooden base blocks (¾" x 6" x 6")
- 1 wooden top block (¾" x 3" x 3")
- wood glue or epoxy
- red, green, and white enamel paint
- 1 magnetic compass
- heavy string

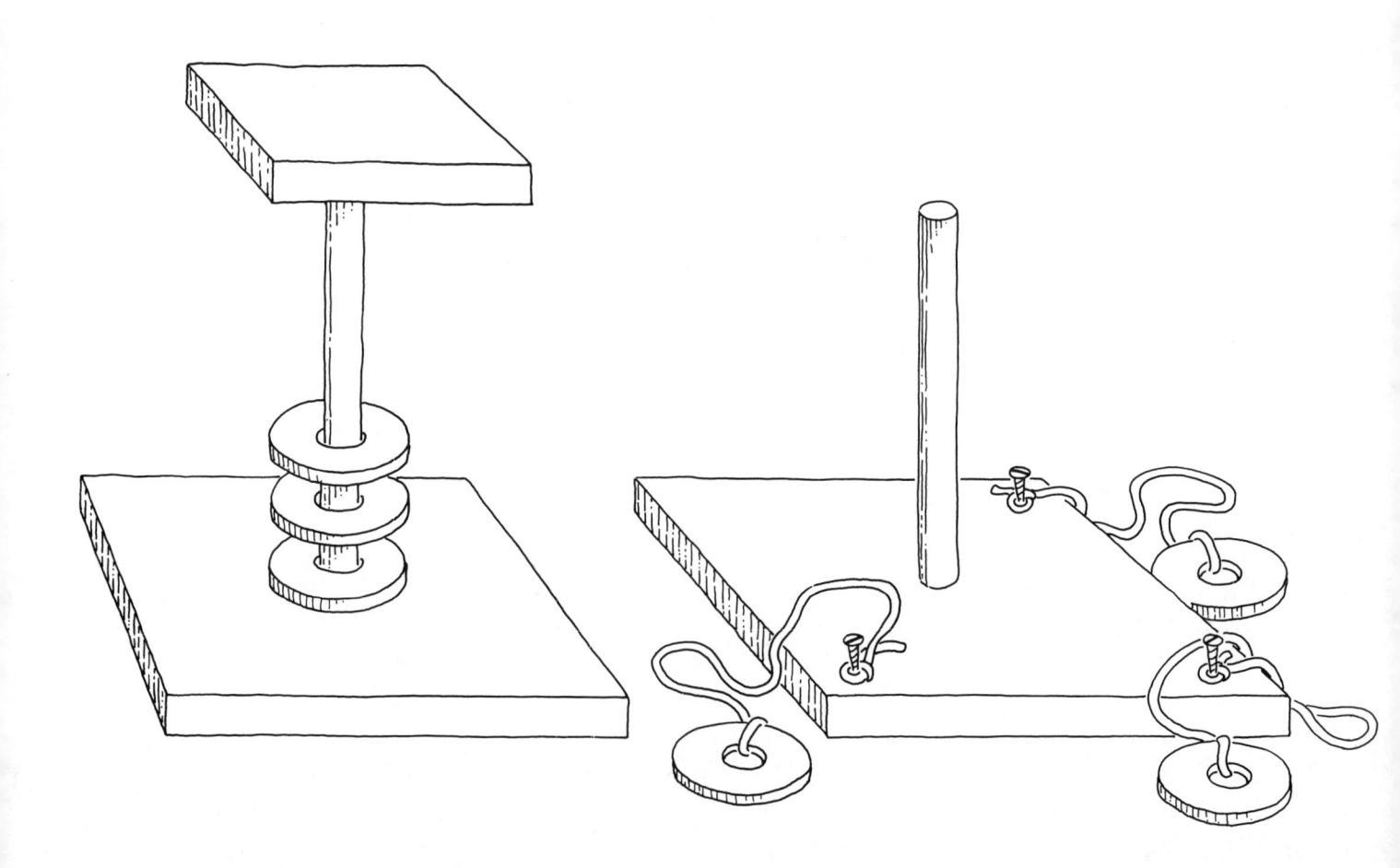

MATERIALS

EXHIBIT
CONSTRUCTION

1. Drill holes in the centers of the top block and the two base blocks. The diameters of the holes must allow the block to be force fit onto the dowel. Paint the base block, dowel, and top block white (or some other color that contrasts with red and green).

2. Glue each of the dowels into the base blocks.

3. Use a compass to identify the north and south poles of three of the ring-shaped magnets. Paint the north poles of the magnets red, and the south poles green. Leave three of the magnets unpainted.

4. Slide three unpainted magnets onto one of the dowels so they "float" above each other. Adjacent magnets will have like poles facing each other.

5. Glue the top block onto the dowel so its corners are oriented the same way as the base block.

6. Tie three of the painted ring-shaped magnets to a nail or screw on the other base block using heavy string. To avoid tangling, the string must be tied to separate corners, just long enough for the rings to go on to the dowel. ▲

The Wizard's FLOATING DISKS

What are these funny disks? What do the red and green colors mean?

Can you make these disks float too?

See if you can get these disks to stay down.

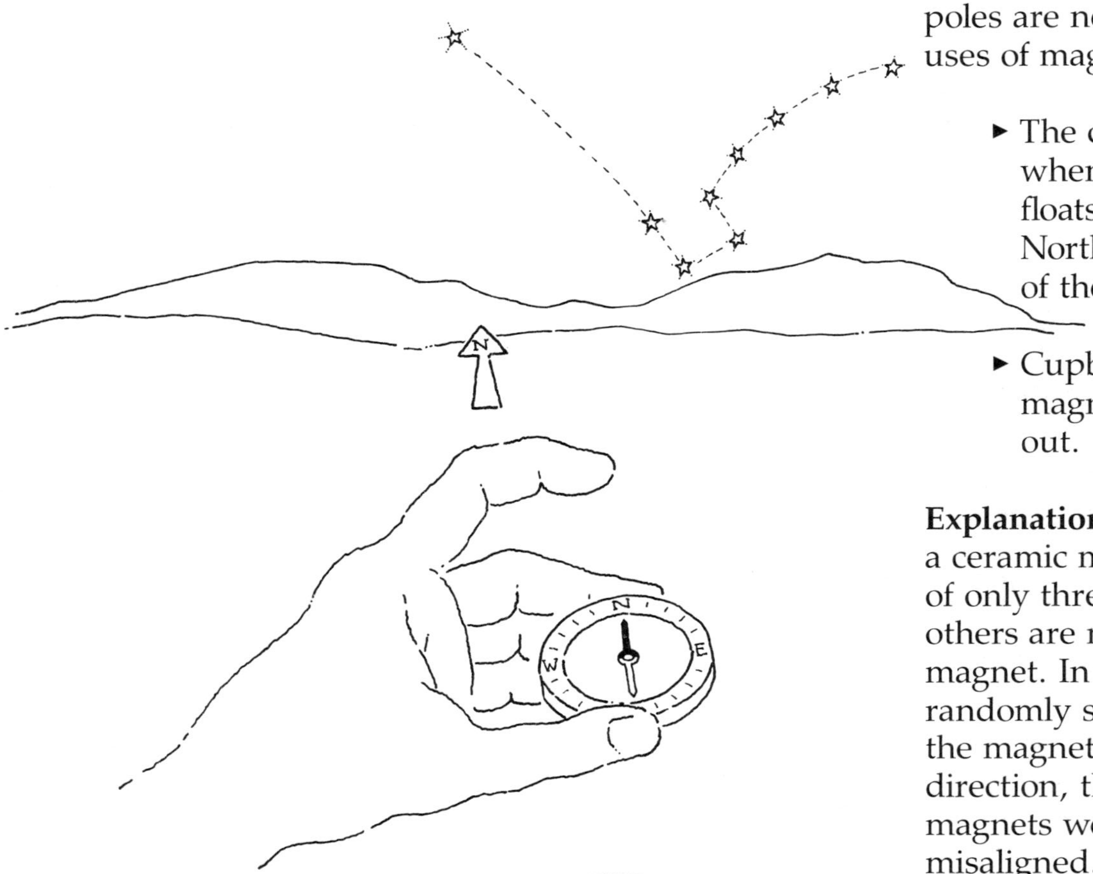

The Wizard's Words About Floating Disks

Applications: Each floating disk is a magnet. Green indicates the south pole of the magnet and red indicates the north pole. Magnets are attracted if opposite poles are near each other. Magnets push each other away if similar poles are near each other. Following are some practical uses of magnets:

▶ The compass was invented thousands of years ago when someone discovered that if a long thin magnet floats freely in a liquid, one end points close to the North Star. That end was called the "north pole" of the magnet.

▶ Cupboard doors and refrigerator doors often use a magnetic latch so there are no moving parts to wear out.

Explanation: The ring magnets in this exhibit are made of a ceramic material with iron embedded in it. Iron is one of only three elements that are naturally magnetic. The others are nickel and cobalt. Each iron atom is a small magnet. In most iron objects, the atoms are oriented randomly so the magnetic forces cancel each other. But if the magnetic poles of many iron atoms point in the same direction, the object is a *permanent magnet*. Permanent magnets weaken with age because the atoms get misaligned. An old magnet can be remagnetized by putting it next to a very strong magnet. ▲

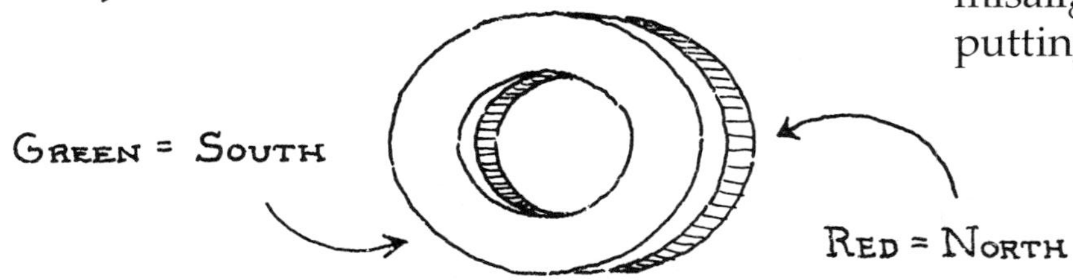

COMPASS NEEDLE POINTS A LITTLE EAST OF NORTH

GREEN = SOUTH

RED = NORTH

EXHIBIT MAINTENANCE

Keep lots of spare magnets on hand, and replace when necessary.

EXHIBIT ▴ GUIDE

MAKERS
·ELECTRICITY·

THE WIZARD'S LAB

▶ELECTRICITY MAKERS

Skills
Observing, Analyzing, Finding Patterns

Concepts
Batteries, Generators, Electricity

Themes
Energy, Matter, Structure,
Systems & Interactions, Models & Simulations

INTRODUCTION

*I*n this exhibit, the visitors are challenged to compare different ways of producing electricity. By connecting wires from an ammeter to different wet cells they are able to compare the efficiency of water vs. vinegar used as an electrolyte. They can also compare the efficiency of steel and aluminum vs. steel and copper as electrode pairs.

Visitors can also make electricity with a magnet and coil of wire. Three coils are provided, allowing visitors to compare the efficiency of coils with different numbers of windings and thicknesses of wire. An additional challenge is to produce electricity with a tiny generator by turning a crank. Visitors who read "The Wizard's Words" learn about how the different devices produce electricity and where they are commonly used. ▲

MATERIALS

- 1 wood baseboard (¾" x 1' x 2' or larger)
- 1 milliammeter, 0 to 5 ma; preferably zero center
- 2 wires, stranded 16 gauge, 18" long, each with alligator clip on one end
- 3 ring magnets (1" diameter)
- 3 sturdy plastic or cardboard tubes, inside diameter slightly greater than the diameter of the magnets, 4" long
- 1 enameled magnet wire, 24 gauge, 100' long
- 1 enameled magnet wire, 24 gauge, 30' long
- 1 enameled magnet wire, 20 gauge, 30' long
- 1 dowel, 6" long with a diameter that fits snugly into the holes of the ring magnets
- 2 paper clips
- 3 sturdy glass or plastic jars with tight-fitting covers
- 3 steel rods (⅛" x 4") or large steel nails for electrodes
- 2 aluminum rods (⅛" x 4") or large aluminum nails for electrodes
- 1 brass or copper rod (⅛" x 4") or large brass bolt for electrode
- 1 DC motor, about 1" diameter, with crank on its shaft
- 1 heavy string, 16" long
- labels
- scraps of wood, paint or varnish, epoxy cement, wood screws, and nails
- solder and soldering iron

EXHIBIT
CONSTRUCTION

Before beginning construction, read the whole section and plan a layout on the baseboard showing where you intend to place each component.

1. Paint, stain, or varnish the baseboard.

2. Mount the three ring magnets in a cluster (with opposite poles together) on one end of the dowel and secure them. One way is to drill 1/16" holes in the dowel. Paper clips can be inserted through the holes and wrapped around the dowel to act as retainers for the cluster of magnets. Drill a 1/8" hole through the other end of the dowel and tie a string through it. The string is fastened to the baseboard near the coils.

3. Wind each length of enameled wire onto a separate tube to form three coils.

4. Use wood to make end retainers for the coils that can secure the ends of the wires as well as provide a means of fastening the coils to the baseboard. Epoxy the end retainers to the coils. The ends of the wires should be soldered onto screws or nails in the end retainers to which the alligator clips can be attached. Sand the nails so the solder makes a good connection. (See diagram.)

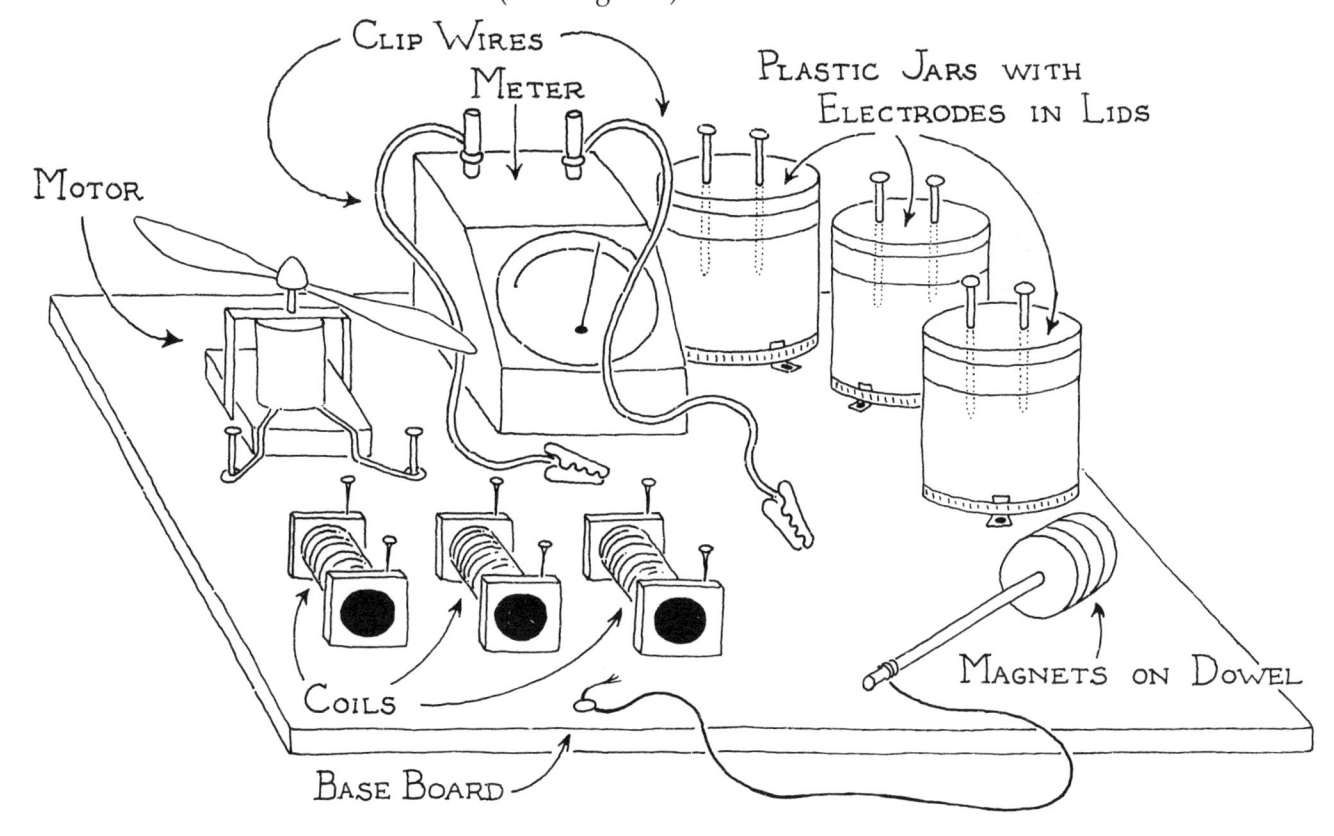

CONSTRUCTION

5. Mount the coils to the baseboard with screws. Drill a hole in the baseboard in the vicinity of the coils and tie the dowel (with magnets) to the baseboard with heavy string. Be sure the placement allows the cluster of magnets to be inserted through each coil of wire. Label the coils:

   a. 300 turns of thin (24 gauge) wire
   b. 100 turns of thin (24 gauge) wire
   c. 100 turns of thicker (20 gauge) wire

6. Mount the three jars on the baseboard. A good mounting method is to use hose clamps attached to small "L" brackets, which are in turn screwed to the baseboard. (While the jars could be glued on with epoxy, that would make changing electrolytes in the jars awkward, requiring you to use a basting bulb or to turn the whole baseboard upside down to empty the jars.)

7. Drill two ⅛" holes in the lid of each jar so the electrode rods can be force fit through the holes. If the lids are made of metal, use plastic electrical tape to insulate the electrodes before fitting them in place. If the lid is too thin to hold the electrodes firmly, attach a small piece of wood to each lid and drill holes through the wood. The holes should be far enough apart so the clip leads attached to each electrode will not short circuit.

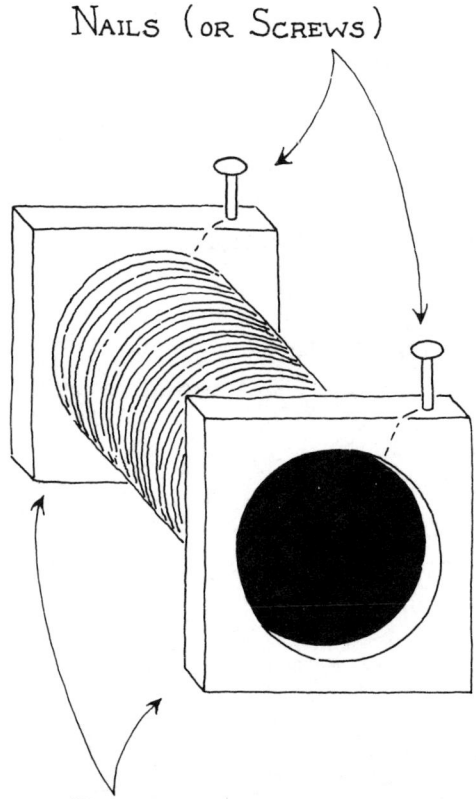

Nails (or Screws)

End Retainers for Coil

CONSTRUCTION

8. Fit the electrode rods into the jar lids so two of the jars each have a steel and an aluminum electrode and the third jar has a steel and a copper electrode. Put labels on the sides of the jars:

   a. steel and aluminum in water
   b. steel and aluminum in vinegar (acid)
   c. steel and copper in water

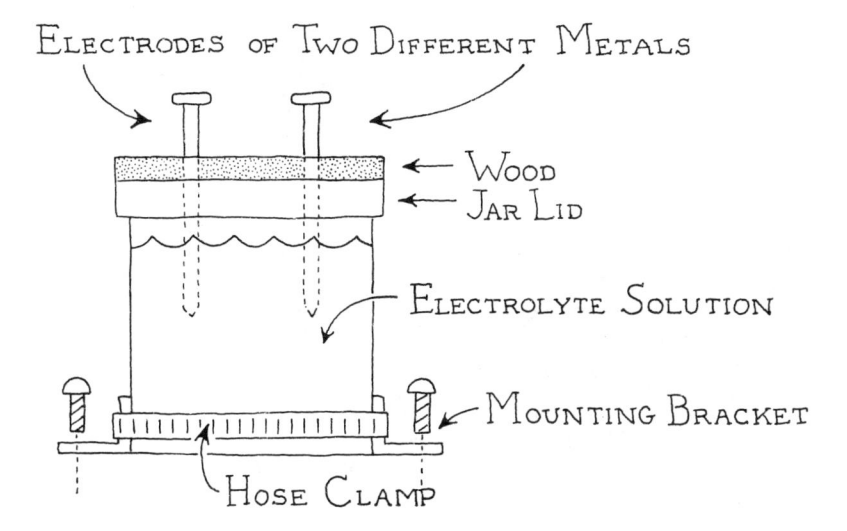

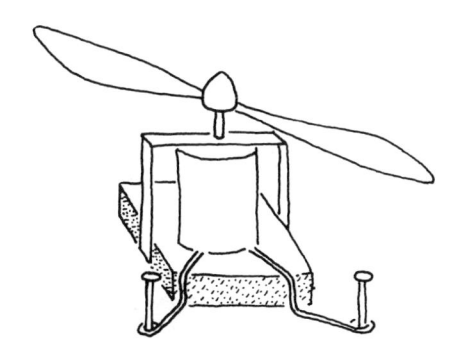

9. Use wood to make a mount for the DC motor so the crank faces up. One way to do this is illustrated in the diagram. Attach the motor wire leads to nails or screws to which alligator clips from the milliammeter can be connected. Be sure these terminals are far enough apart to avoid short circuiting by the alligator clips touching each other.

10. Mount the milliammeter to the base board. Permanently attach wires with alligator clips on the ends to each terminal of the milliammeter.

11. Fill the three plastic jars with electrolytes according to the labels: two jars with water and one with vinegar. Dilute the vinegar by adding 7 parts water to 1 part vinegar. ▲

CONSTRUCTION

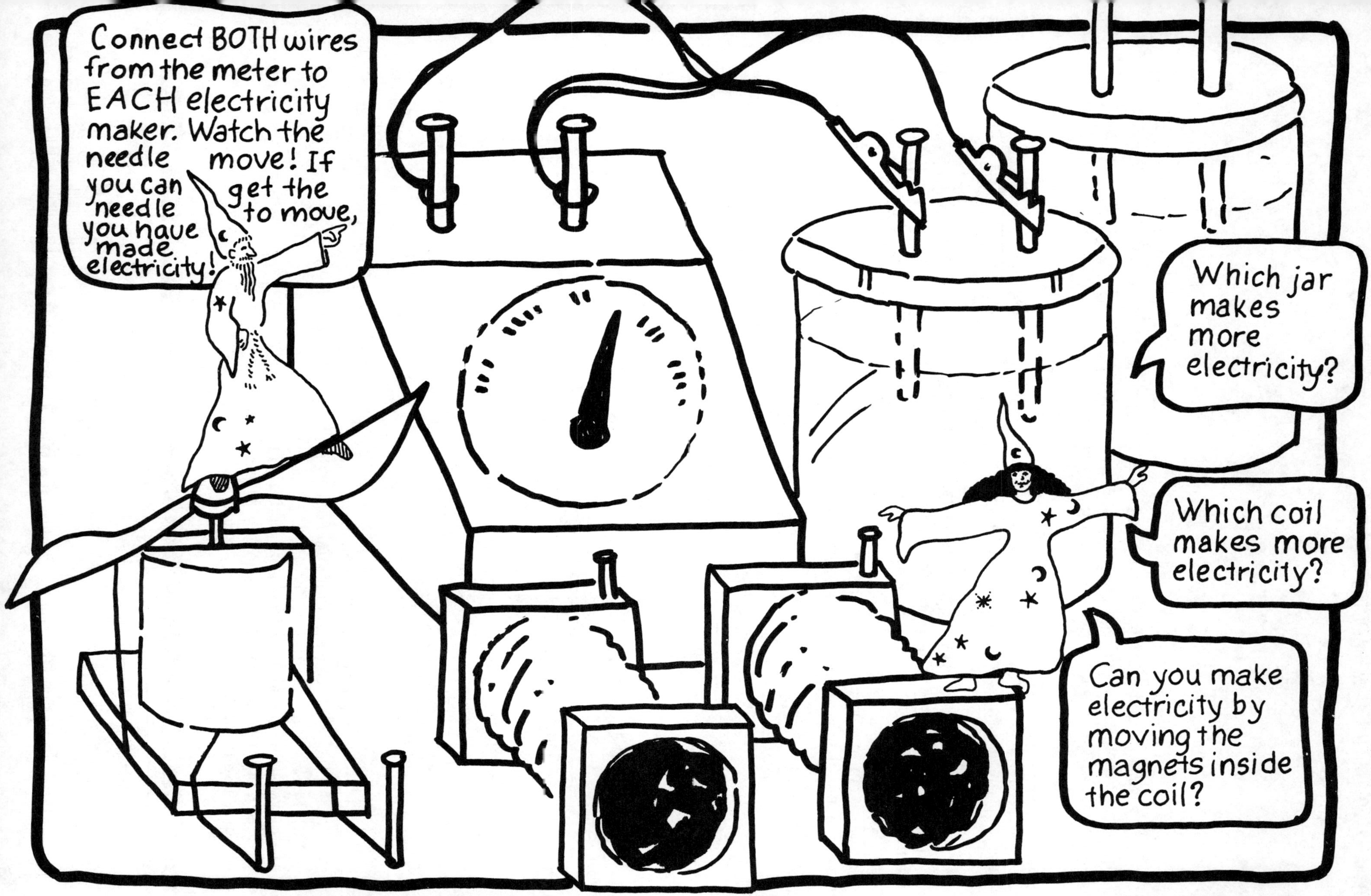

The WIZARD'S ELECTRICITY MAKERS

Connect BOTH wires from the meter to EACH electricity maker. Watch the needle move! If you can get the needle to move, you have made electricity!

Can you make electricity by moving the magnets inside the coil?

Which coil makes more electricity?

Which jar makes more electricity?

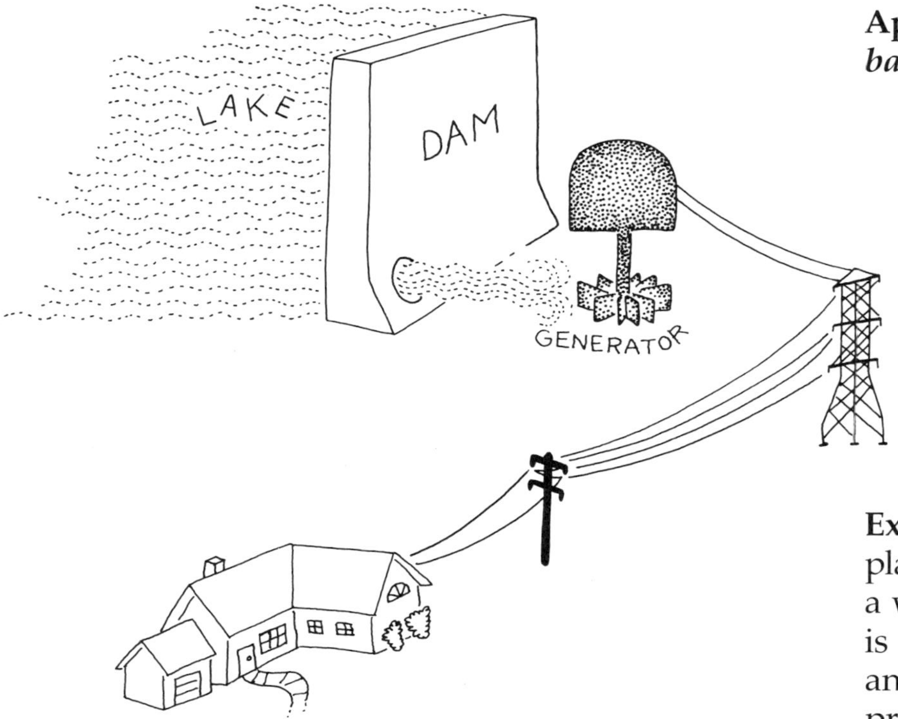

The Wizard's Words About Electricity Makers

Application: Each electricity maker on the board is a *battery* or a *generator.*

▶ We use batteries to provide electricity for flashlights and tape recorders.

▶ Electricity for home lighting and heating is produced by a generator. The generator may be run by water power, wind, or steam. Steam may be produced by burning coal or oil, collecting sunlight with mirrors, tapping hot underground springs, or by a nuclear reactor.

Explanation of Batteries: When two different metals are placed into certain kinds of liquid and connected with a wire, a stream of electrons flows through the wire. This is called an *electric current.* The liquid is the *electrolyte* and the metal pieces are *electrodes.* Which electrodes produce more electricity, steel and aluminum, or steel and copper? Which electrolyte produces more electric current, water or vinegar?

Explanation of Generators: Moving a magnet near a wire also causes electrons to flow and makes the meter needle move. You can experiment by moving the magnet back and forth inside the coils. Which produces more electric current, a coil with fewer turns or more turns? A coil of thick wire or thin wire? The tiny generator with the crank has a magnet and coil of wire inside. Connect wires from the meter to it and try turning the crank by hand. Does the amount of electricity depend on which way you turn it? ▲

EXHIBIT MAINTENANCE

1. Some DC motors have fragile lead wires that must be protected from being broken or yanked out of their sockets. One way to do this is to wrap the lead wires around the body of the motor once or twice and tape them tightly with a piece of electrical tape, thus relieving stress on the places where the wires connect into the motor.

2. The electrolytes get dirty after a time and should be changed.

3. The electrodes accumulate scale deposits or are eaten away, depending on whether they are positive or negative. Keep spare electrodes on hand for replacement.

4. Eventually the motor wears out, so have spares on hand.

5. We recommend fairly heavy gauge wire for the alligator leads. Nonetheless, the wire can break and the alligator clips may come off. Have spares on hand. ▲

EXHIBIT ▲ GUIDE

HUMAN BATTERY

THE WIZARD'S LAB

HUMAN BATTERY

Skills
Observing, Analyzing, Finding Patterns

Concepts
Batteries, Electrodes, Electrolytes, Electricity

Themes
Energy, Matter, Structure,
Systems & Interactions, Models & Simulations

INTRODUCTION

This exhibit produces electric current, using the visitor as part of the electric wet cell. When the visitor touches two electrodes he observes a small voltage on a voltmeter. The visitor can compare the amount of voltage that is produced by touching pairs of electrodes made from different metals.

"The Wizard's Words" gives examples of electric charges commonly generated by living things and offers a brief description of a wet cell. The explanation notes that in this exhibit no liquid is provided for an electrolyte and asks, "Guess who supplies the liquid? (Remember, humans are 90% salt water!)" ▲

MATERIALS

- 1 wood baseboard (¾" x 12" x 12")
- 6 metal plates (3" x 3") made from: zinc, aluminum, brass, steel, and two made from copper.
- 1 microammeter, zero center
- stranded wire, 16 gauge, 36" long
- wood scraps and screws as needed

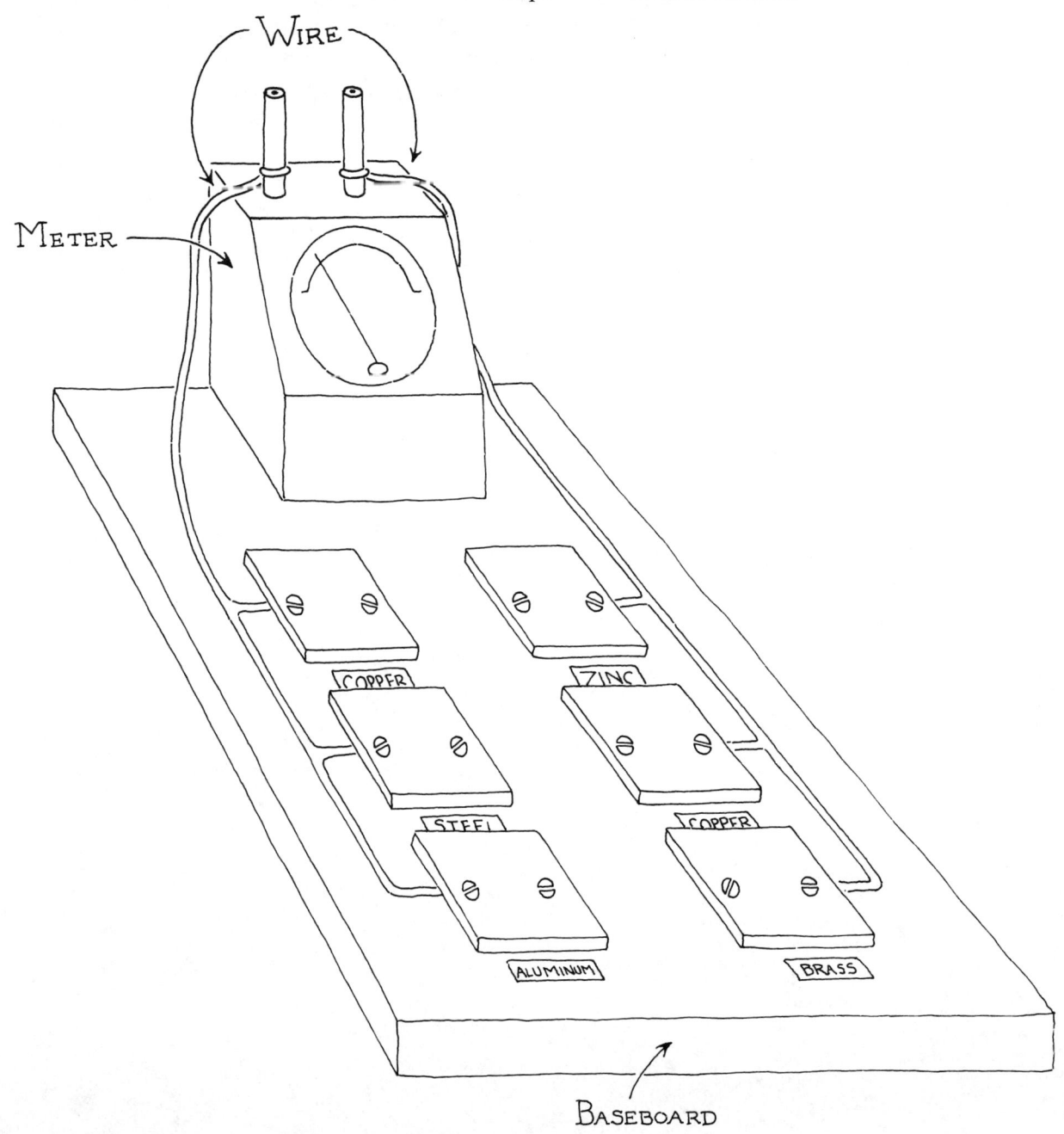

EXHIBIT
CONSTRUCTION

1. Paint, stain, or varnish the baseboard.

2. Attach the metal plates to the baseboard with wood screws, as shown in the picture. Don't tighten the screws all the way yet.

3. Mount the microammeter on the baseboard with wood screws.

4. Cut connecting wires to proper lengths so they extend from the terminals of the microammeter to the metal plates, as shown in the picture.

5. Strip the ends of the wires and secure them to their respective terminals and plates. Strip off enough insulation to secure the wires to the plates by wrapping the stripped ends around the wood screws and then tightening the screws all the way.

6. Label all plates with the name of the metal they are made from. ▲

The Wizard's HUMAN BATTERY

ZOWIE! What an electric personality you have!

Which pair of metals produce the most electricity?

Press on each pair of plates and watch the needle on the voltmeter.

The Wizard's Words About The Human Battery

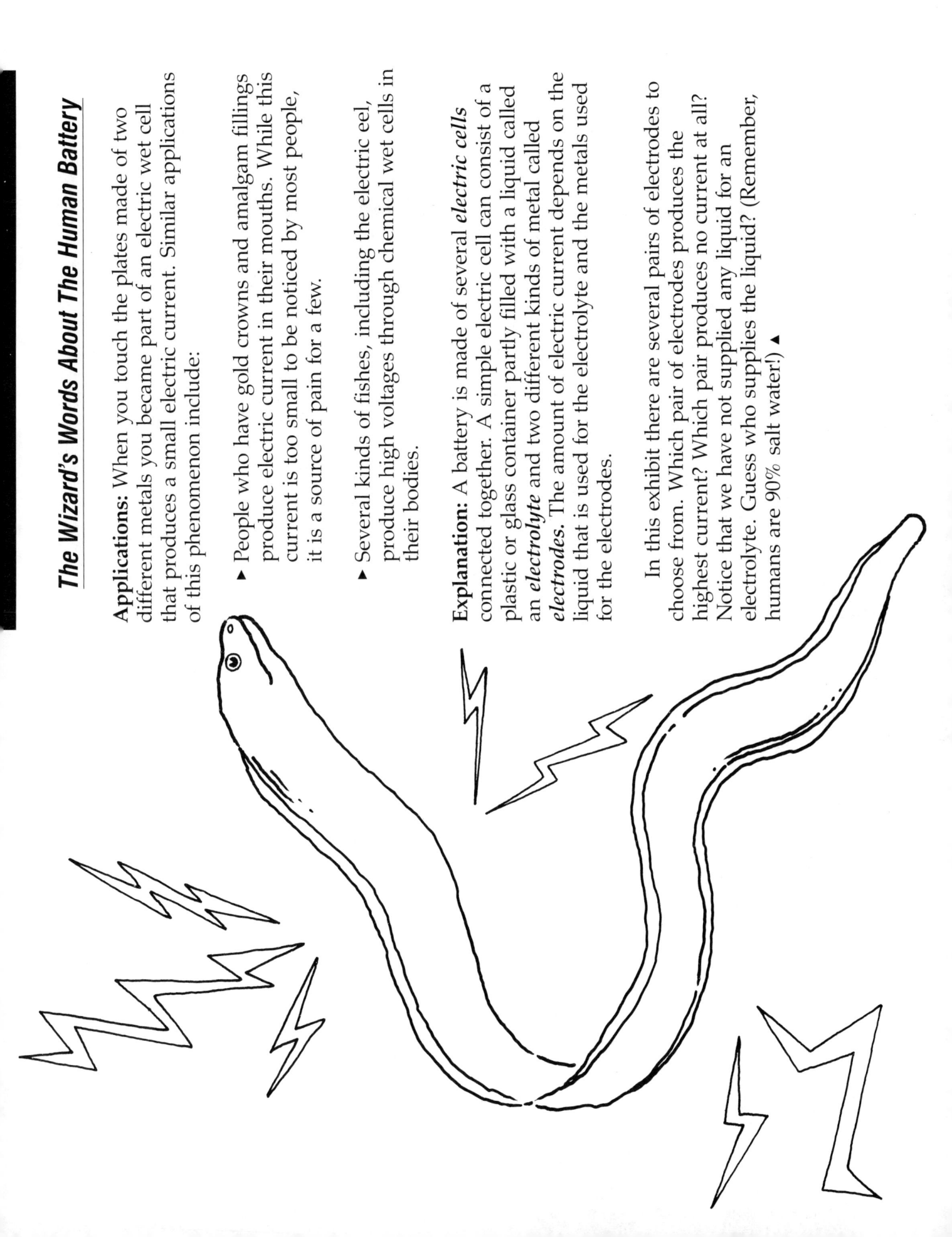

Applications: When you touch the plates made of two different metals you became part of an electric wet cell that produces a small electric current. Similar applications of this phenomenon include:

▶ People who have gold crowns and amalgam fillings produce electric current in their mouths. While this current is too small to be noticed by most people, it is a source of pain for a few.

▶ Several kinds of fishes, including the electric eel, produce high voltages through chemical wet cells in their bodies.

Explanation: A battery is made of several *electric cells* connected together. A simple electric cell can consist of a plastic or glass container partly filled with a liquid called an *electrolyte* and two different kinds of metal called *electrodes*. The amount of electric current depends on the liquid that is used for the electrolyte and the metals used for the electrodes.

In this exhibit there are several pairs of electrodes to choose from. Which pair of electrodes produces the highest current? Which pair produces no current at all? Notice that we have not supplied any liquid for an electrolyte. Guess who supplies the liquid? (Remember, humans are 90% salt water!) ▲

EXHIBIT MAINTENANCE

1. Fasten the wires to the baseboard to prevent people from grabbing and yanking them out.

2. The metal plates will develop oxide coatings after a few days of use. Clean them with emery paper or steel wool.

3. Keep a replacement microammeter on hand in case the one on the exhibit breaks. Replace wires if they break. ▲

EXHIBIT▲GUIDE

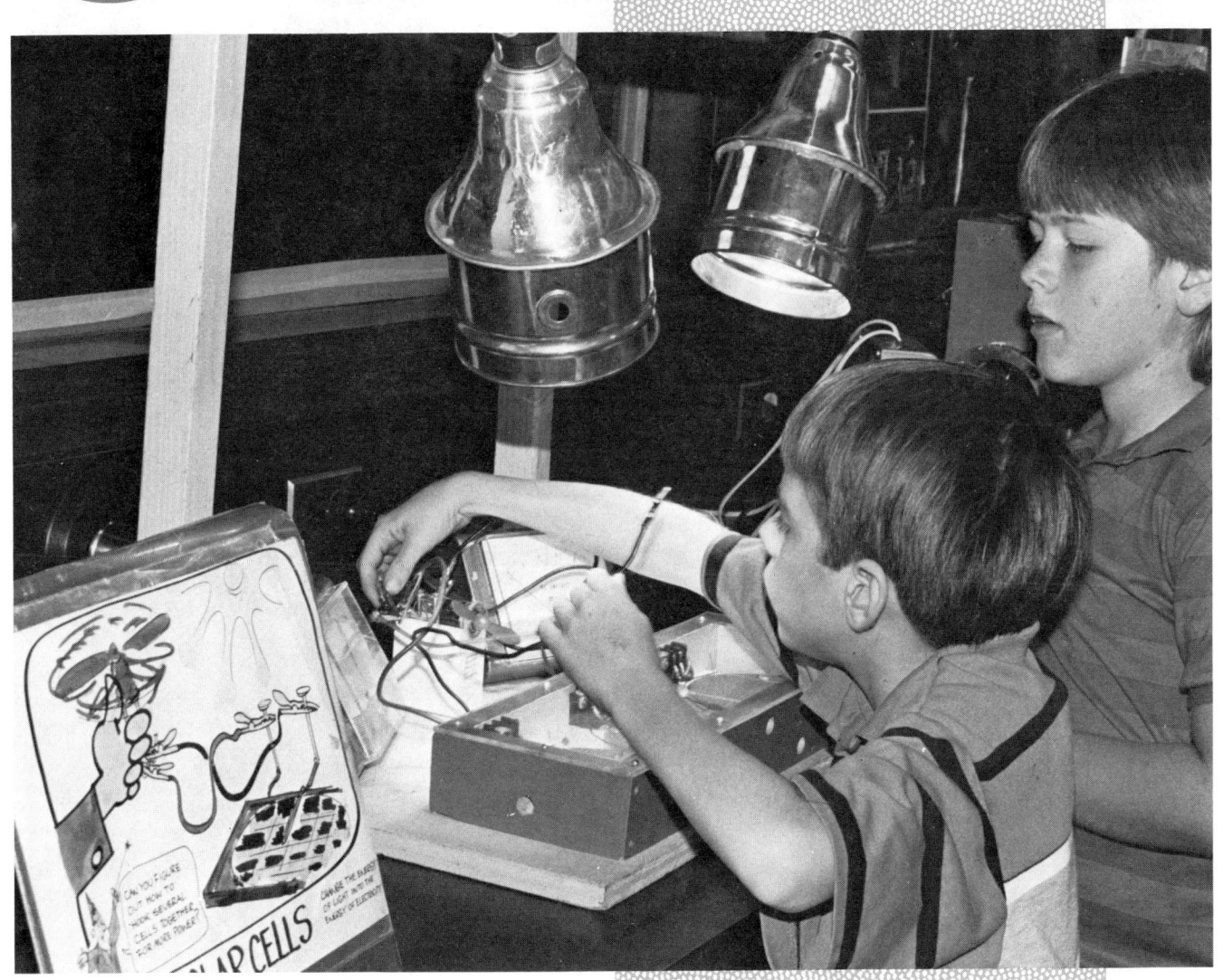

S**C**O**E**L**L**A**L**R**S**

THE WIZARD'S LAB

SOLAR CELLS

Skills
Observing, Analyzing, Finding Patterns

Concepts
Solar Energy, Solar Cells, Light, Series and Parallel Circuits

Themes
Energy, Matter, Structure,
Systems & Interactions, Models & Simulations

INTRODUCTION

Solar cells—also called *photovoltaics*—convert light energy directly to electrical energy. These devices are becoming an increasingly attractive source of electric power for many applications. In this exhibit visitors experiment with three solar cells. The cells have wires attached that allow the visitor to connect them together in series and in parallel circuits. The visitors are also provided with a voltmeter, an ammeter, a calculator, and a small electric motor to compare the electricity generated by the different circuits.

When visitors succeed in setting up a circuit that moves the needle on a meter or runs the motor, they can shade the cells with their hands and observe the resulting loss of current. A calculator on the board illustrates a practical application of solar cells. Those who read "The Wizard's Words" find a brief explanation of how solar cells convert light to electrical energy. ▲

MATERIALS

- 1 wood baseboard (¾" x 12" x 18")
- 2 wood frame pieces (¾" x 2" x 6")
- 2 wood frame pieces (¾" x 2" x 16")
- 1 clear plastic sheet (¼" x 16" x 7½")
- 3 solar cells, 4" diameter (available through scientific companies or electronics stores)
- 1 calculator powered by solar cells
- 1 ammeter: −2 to +2 ampere (zero center preferable)
- 1 voltmeter: −2 to +2 volts (zero center preferable)
- 1 DC motor: about 1" diameter, with propeller on shaft
- 3 red wires, 16 gauge stranded, 18" long
- 3 black wires, 16 gauge stranded, 18" long
- 3 red wires, 20 gauge stranded, 6" long
- 3 black wires, 20 gauge stranded, 6" long
- 6 alligator clips
- 1 adjustable lamp with 150-watt floodlight
- 3 terminal strips, 2 lug
- 1 tube of silicone cement
- wood scraps and screws as needed
- paint or varnish
- solder and solder iron with adjustable heat level

59

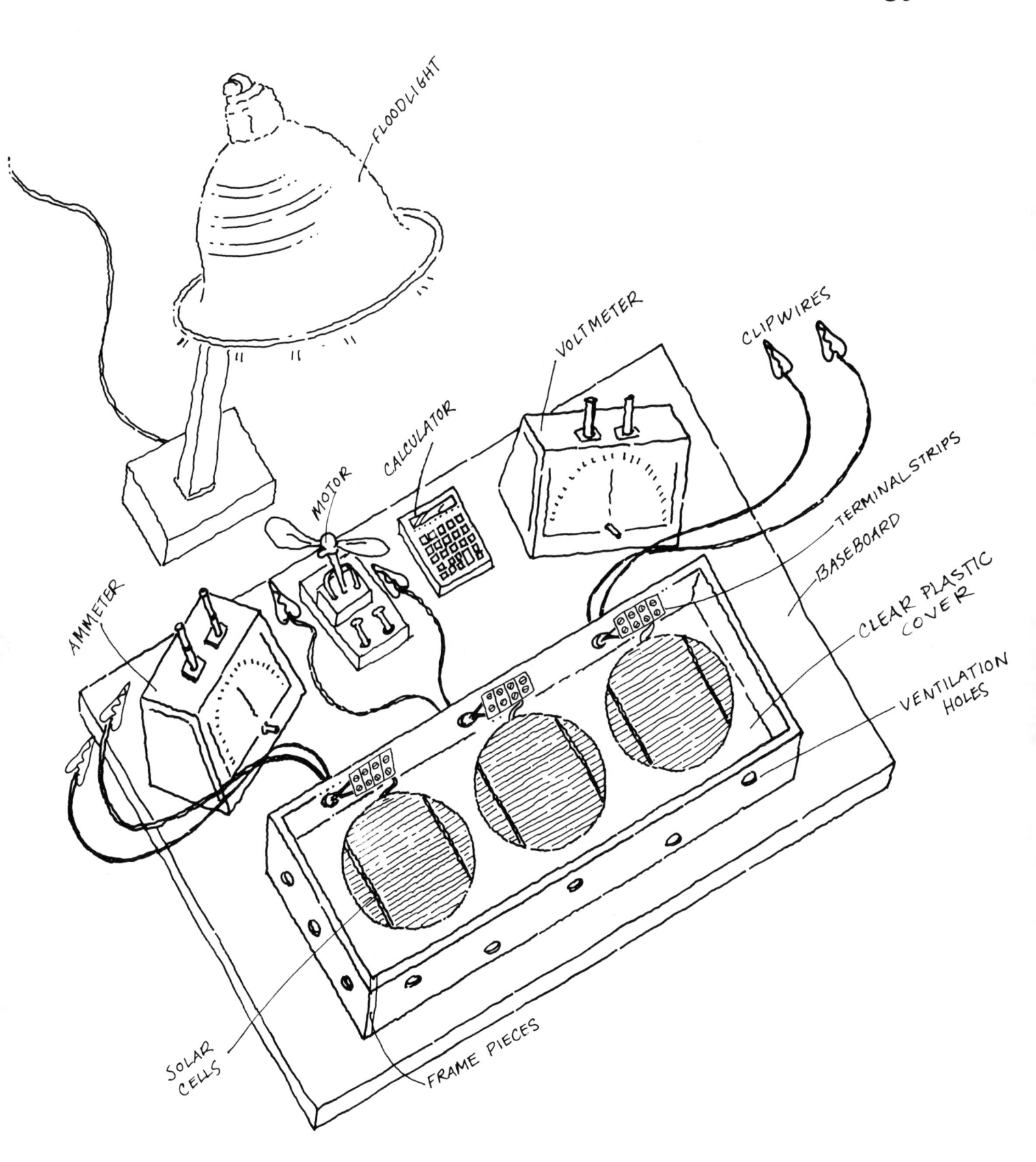

EXHIBIT
CONSTRUCTION

1. Read this entire section first. Then plan the layout of the baseboard and paint or varnish the baseboard.

2. Drill ⅜" cooling holes at about 4" intervals in the frame pieces. Drill the holes near the bottoms of the 2" faces (holes will be ¾" deep).

3. Mount three terminal strips on one of the longer frame wood pieces where the three solar cells will be located and drill a ⅜" hole near each terminal strip for a pair of wires to pass through.

4. Screw the frame wood pieces to the baseboard in a rectangle near one edge of the baseboard as shown in the diagram. The terminal strips must be on the wood piece closest to the center of the baseboard, on the inside of the rectangle.

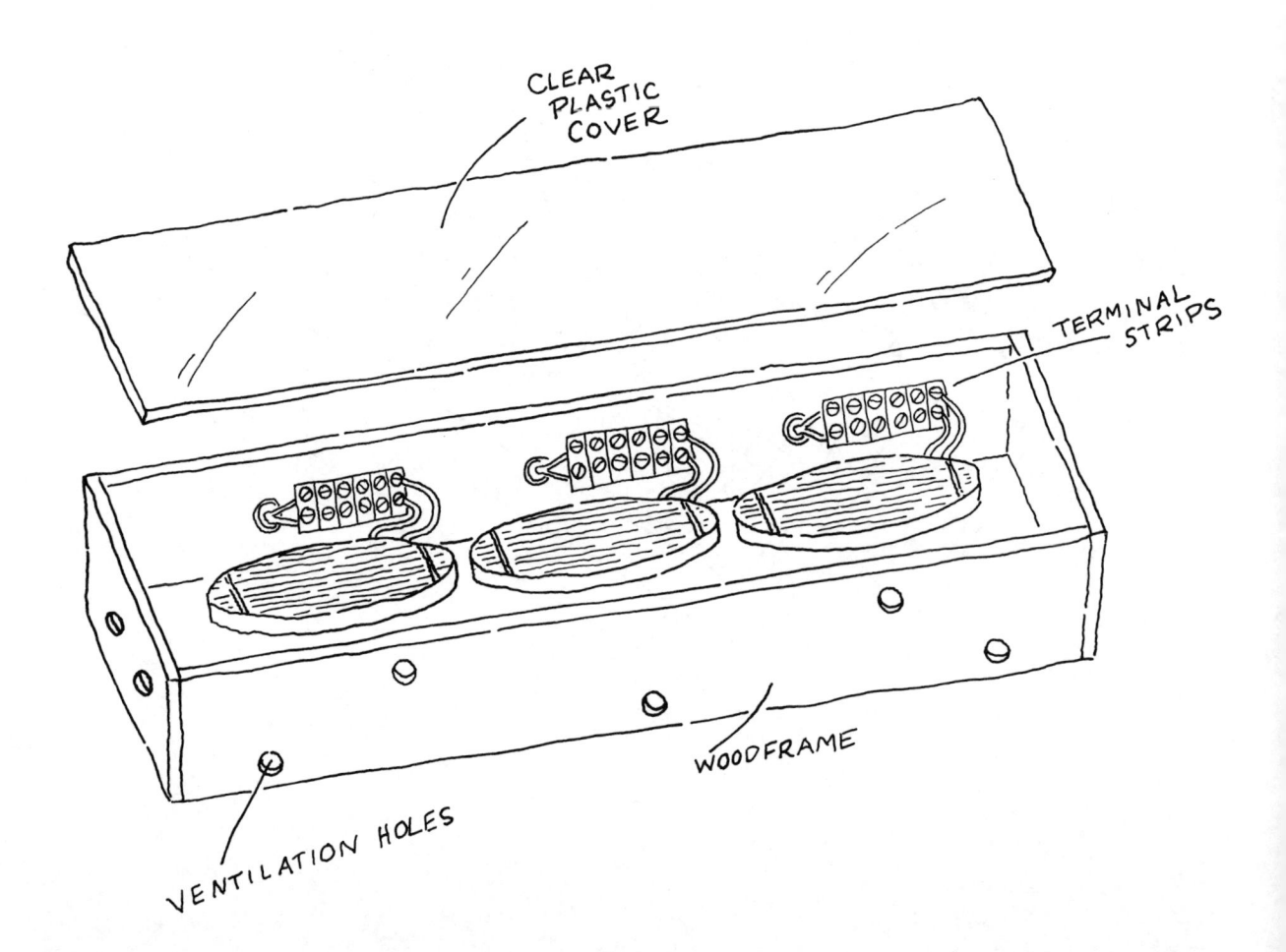

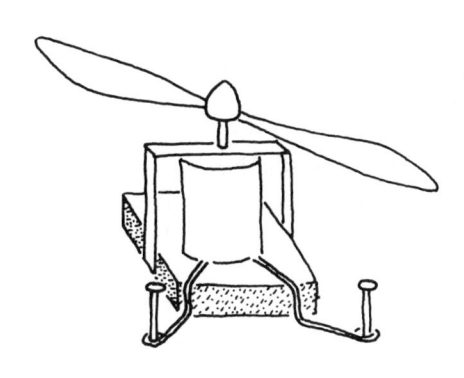

5. Glue some small pieces of wood to the baseboard inside the rectangle to elevate the solar cells above the baseboard. These pieces should be about ¾" thick. The solar cells must not press against the plastic cover.

6. Use small pieces of wood to make a mounting stand for the DC motor and secure it to the baseboard. Attach the motor's lead wires to terminal nails or screws to which clips leads may be easily connected.

7. Mount the voltmeter, ammeter, and solar calculator on the baseboard facing where the solar cells will be.

8. Attach an 18" red wire and an 18" black wire to each terminal strip (on separate lugs). Pass the end of each wire through one of the holes made in step 3 before attaching to the terminal strip.

9. Solder an alligator clip to the other end of each wire.

CONSTRUCTION

10. Solder wires to solar cells. **Caution 1:** Solar cells are extremely fragile; handle with care. **Caution 2:** Avoid getting fingerprints on them, especially on the top (dark) surface. **Caution 3:** To avoid heat damage to solar cells use a low temperature soldering iron (not more than 25 Watt or 275°–300°C.) With these cautions in mind, connect a red wire and a black wire from each solar cell to the nearest terminal strip, making sure the colors of the solar cell wires match the colors of the long wires already soldered on each lug. Most solar cells have obvious spots where wires are to be soldered. Using a meter and a light source, verify which point of the solar cell is positive and which is negative. Follow the usual convention of connecting red wires for positive and black wires for negative. Trim the lengths of the wires before making final solder connections to make a neat and attractive wiring job.

11. Use silicone to cement the solar cells to the support blocks inside the rectangle on the baseboard.

12. Place the clear plastic over the wood rectangle and mark spots on the acrylic plastic to drill ⅜" ventilation/cooling holes. Do not locate any holes directly above any solar cell to prevent visitors from poking objects like pens or pencils directly onto the cells and damaging them. Also mark places to drill holes for wood screws to secure the clear plastic to the frame. The screws should be spaced fairly close together (not more than 4" apart) to prevent warping of the plastic due to heat from the floodlight.

13. Remove the clear plastic from over the solar cells and drill the holes as marked. Screw the acrylic plastic in place over the solar cells.

14. Adjust the lamp so all three cells are illuminated. It is a good idea to extend the aluminum reflector on the floodlight with a cylindrical metal piece in order to: 1) concentrate more light onto the solar cells; 2) prevent people from touching the hot floodlight bulbs; and 3) absorb heat from the existing reflectors to keep the lights from getting too hot. ▲

The WIZARD'S SOLAR CELLS

Can you figure out how to hook several cells together to make the propeller turn?

What happens when you block the light?

To see how much electricity solar cells can make from light shining on them, connect the cells to the electric meters.

The Wizard's Words About Solar Cells

Applications: Solar cells convert light directly to electricity. Here are some examples of how they are used:

▶ Solar cells have been used to provide electric power in remote locations. The electricity is stored in large batteries during the day so the power can be used at night.

▶ Solar cells are used to power radios, battery chargers, music boxes, calculators, home appliances, cars, space satellites, and even an airplane!

Explanation: A solar cell is a thin slice of a silicon crystal that has a small amount of an impurity embedded in one side, and a different impurity on the other side. The impurities create an excess of electrons on one side of the crystal, and a shortage of electrons on the other side. A wire is connected to each side. In this exhibit you can connect the wires through a meter or motor. When light falls on the cell, electrons flow through the wires from the side with excess electrons to the side with a shortage of electrons, thus creating an electric current.

In a *parallel circuit*, the positive terminals are connected and the negative terminals are connected. In a *series circuit*, the positive terminal of one cell is connected to the negative terminal of the next. Which type of circuit (series or parallel) increases current only? Which type increases voltage? Does one type of circuit make the motor spin faster? ◀

EXHIBIT MAINTENANCE

1. Light bulbs will need to be replaced and wires may break and need to be repaired.

2. The meters may eventually wear out or need replacing.

3. The DC motor can wear out. Keep spares on hand. A sluggish DC motor can often be restored by placing a tiny drop of lightweight oil on each end of the spindle and letting the oil flow into the bearings. ▲

EXHIBIT GUIDE

LENSES

THE WIZARD'S LAB

►LENSES

Skills
Observing, Analyzing, Finding Patterns

Concepts
Lens Focal Length, Lens Curvature, Focal Point, Light, Images

Themes
Systems & Interactions, Energy, Matter, Structure, Scale

INTRODUCTION

*M*any people enjoy playing with lenses and light. This exhibit invites visitors to compare the images produced by lenses of different curvatures. The cartoon Wizard also challenges the visitors to find two different images formed by one lens—a small image like that formed by a camera lens, and a large image like that projected by a slide projector. "The Wizard's Words" explain how lenses function to form images and why those images are upside down. ▲

MATERIALS

- 1 meter stick
- 2 wood boards (½" x 12" x 40")
- 3 wood endboards (¾" x 10" x 10")
- 1 socket with wall plug and switch
- 1 100-watt frosted light bulb
- 1 white translucent plastic panel (⅛" x 10" x 10")
- 1 piece of clear plastic (¼" x 10" x 10")
- 1 lens, about 10 cm focal length, at least 3 cm diameter
- 1 lens, about 25 cm focal length, same diameter as above
- scrap wood to make lens cells
- black and white latex paint
- clear lacquer
- red and green string
- red and green cellophane, theatrical gels, or felt-tip markers that will write on plastic
- wood screws and glue as needed
- epoxy cement

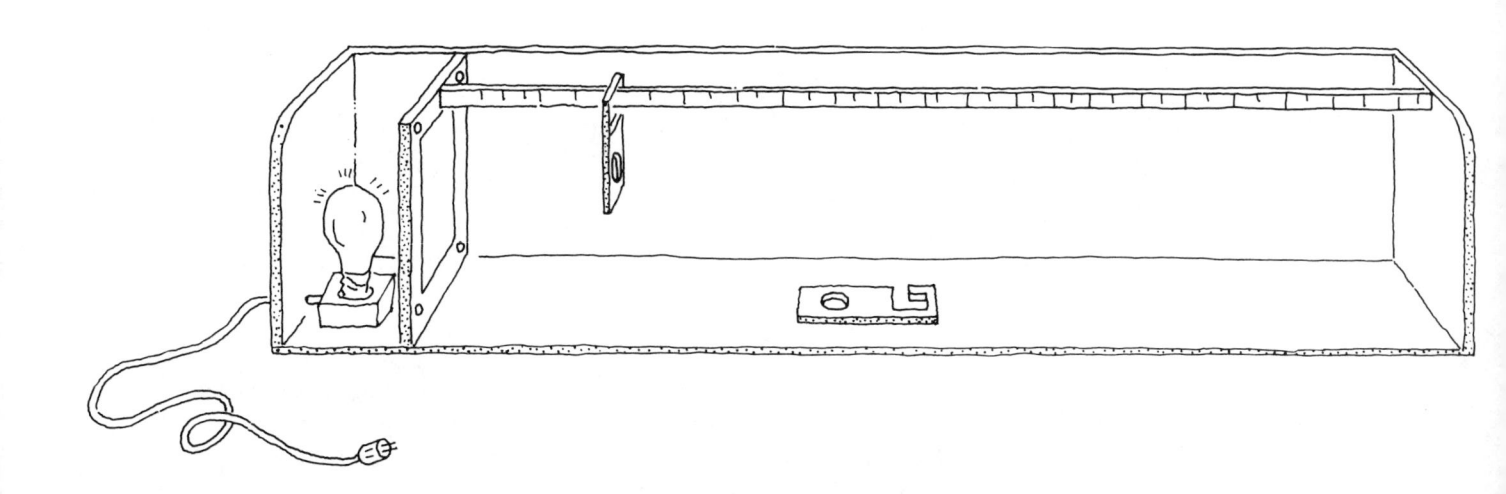

EXHIBIT
CONSTRUCTION

1. Drill holes into the ends of the meter stick. The diameter of the hole should be slightly under the thread size of the wood screws.

2. Cut the boards as shown in the diagram.

3. Cut a "window" out of one end board as shown in the diagram. Cut a sheet of translucent white plastic and a sheet of clear plastic the same size as the end board. Color the top of the white plastic red and the bottom part green by taping on sheets of colored cellophane or theatrical gels, or by using permanent felt-tipped markers. Write the word "Focus" in the middle. The word "Focus" should read frontwards when viewed from the bulb side of the exhibit. It will appear backwards when viewed from the other side. Screw the pieces together. Drill a hole in the top centers of the boards for attaching the meter stick.

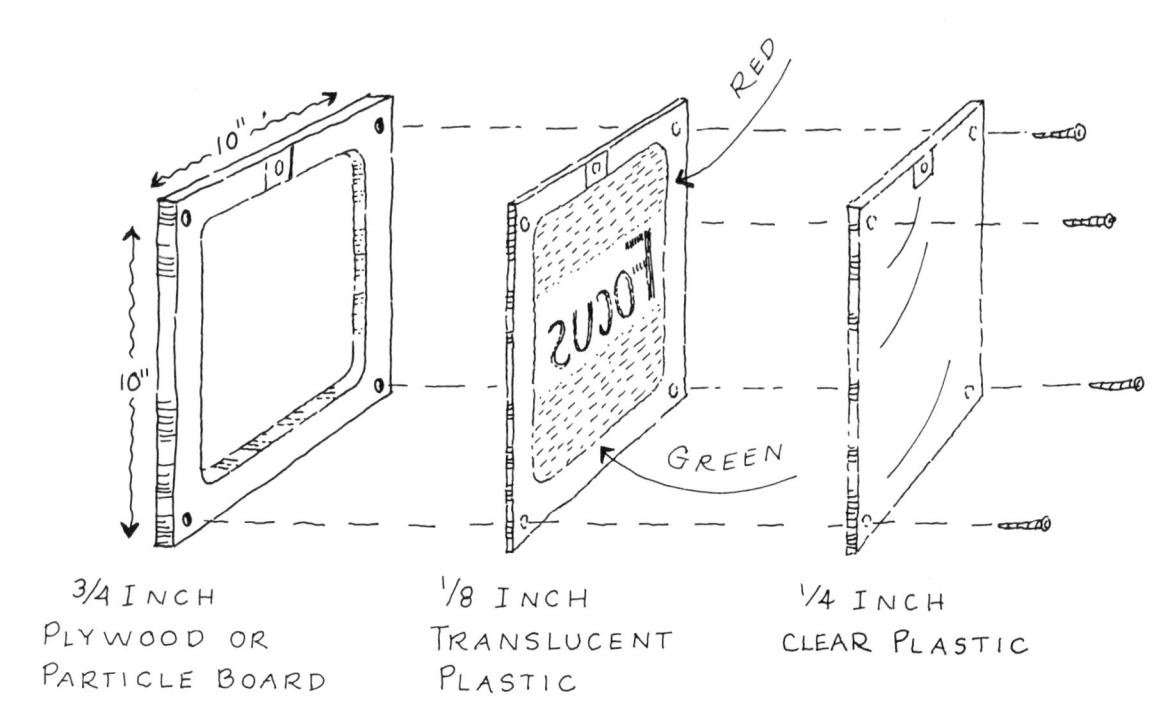

3/4 INCH PLYWOOD OR PARTICLE BOARD

1/8 INCH TRANSLUCENT PLASTIC

1/4 INCH CLEAR PLASTIC

4. Install the light socket on the bottom of the baseboard. In order to prevent visitors from burning their fingers, the bulb should be enclosed behind plastic or wood. Attach with screws so the bulb can be replaced. Drill ventilation/cooling holes in the bulb enclosure.

5. Secure the endboards to the baseboard and back panel with screws.

6. Paint with white latex the area around the light socket and inner side of the endboard where images will be projected. Paint the rest of the exhibit black.

7. Create graphics on the back panel: Stretch red and green string to represent light rays from the red and green areas of the lighted panel, through a piece of wood or plastic shaped like a lens, to the screen where the image will be projected. Be careful to place Wizard C, who asks, "which lens focuses an image when you put it here?" at the location where one of the lenses will form an image on the screen. Add Wizard cartoons and speaking bubbles as shown in the diagram on pages 6 and 7. Paint or spray with clear lacquer.

8. Attach the meter stick between the end pieces with screws.

9. Make lens mounts that can hang from the meter stick. The "hook" part should be long enough to allow the lens to hang at the same height as the center of the lighted panel. Cement the lenses in place with epoxy.

10. Label the long focal length lens "LESS CURVED LENS" and the short focal length lens "MORE CURVED LENS." ▲

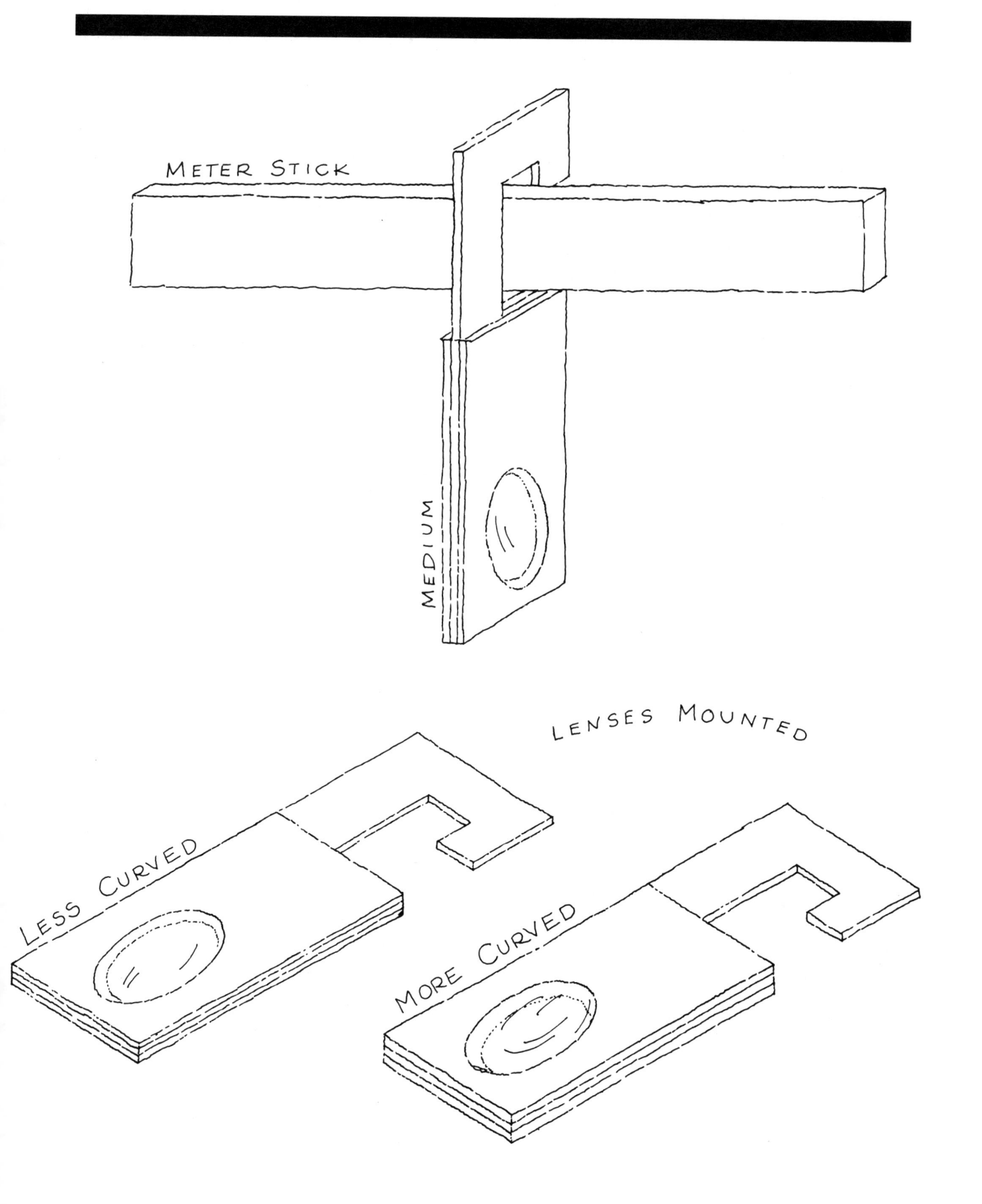

METER STICK

MEDIUM

LENSES MOUNTED

LESS CURVED

MORE CURVED

A. Hang just one lens on the meter stick.

B. Slide the lens back and forth along the stick. Watch the screen. Can you see the image appear?

D. How are the images different from the original picture?

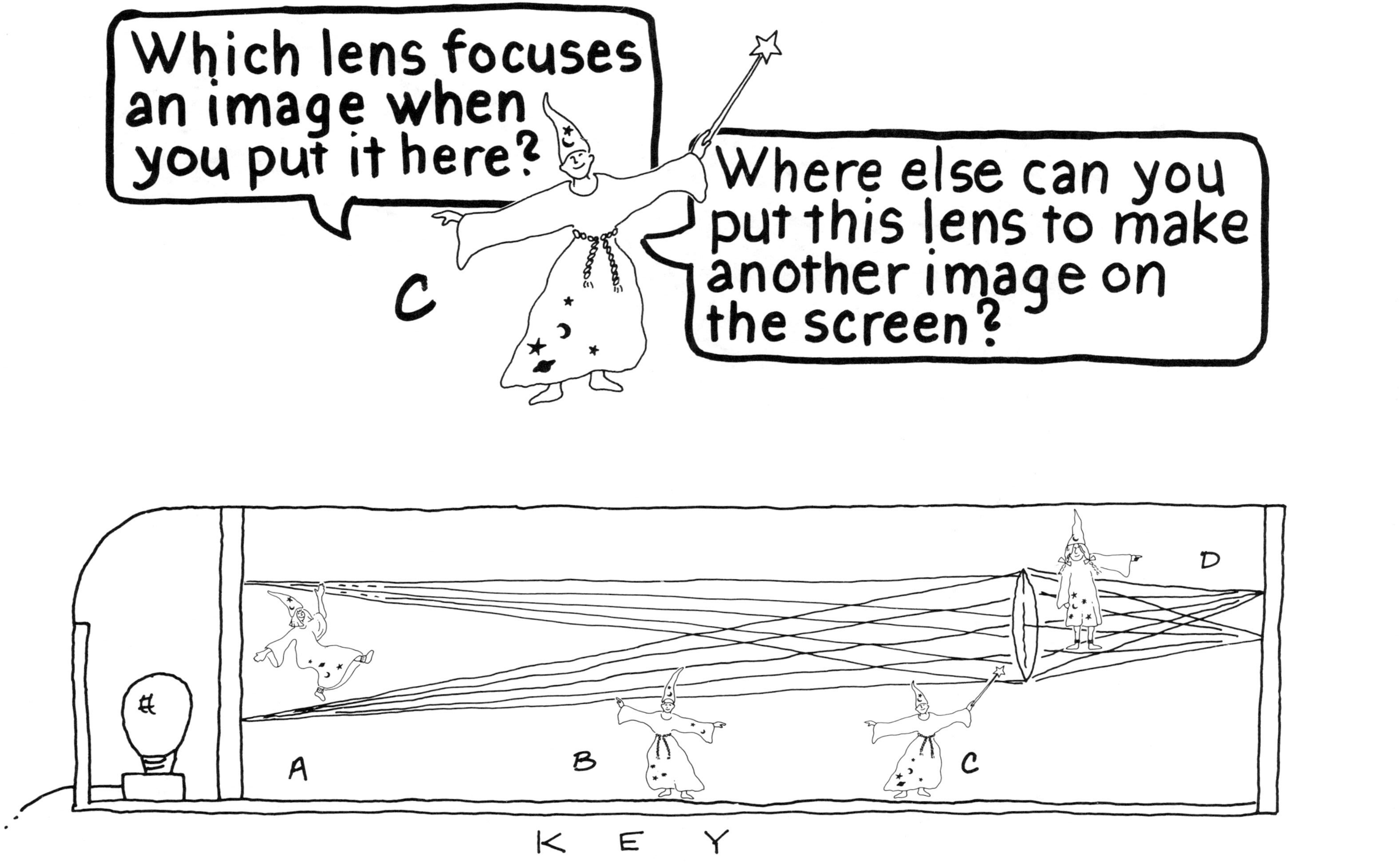
Which lens focuses an image when you put it here?
C
Where else can you put this lens to make another image on the screen?
A
B
C
D
KEY

The Wizard's LENSES

Hang one lens on the stick. Slide it back and forth.

Watch the screen. Can you make a picture or image appear?

Are the images right-side up or upside down?

The Wizard's Words About Lenses

Applications: Lenses are used in microscopes, telescopes, binoculars, cameras, slide projectors, eyeglasses, and many other instruments. The lenses in this exhibit form pictures or *images* of the lighted panel, much as they do in the following instruments:

▶ **Cameras**—You probably noticed that when a lens in this exhibit is placed a little way from the white screen, it forms a small upside down image. This is very much like the image formed by a camera lens on film. Which lens takes a bigger "picture?"

▶ **Slide Projectors**—As you move a lens closer to the brightly-lit panel you will find a position where it projects a large image onto the white screen. This is like the image of a slide created by a projector lens. Which lens projects a bigger view of the "slide?"

Explanation: Light rays usually travel in straight lines, but it is not difficult to make them bend. Place a clear material such as glass at an angle in front of the oncoming light. The greater the angle, the more the light will bend. A glass lens is curved so that light rays striking the lens near the center are bent very little, while rays closer to the edge enter the glass at a greater angle and so are bent more. The smooth curvature of a lens bends the light rays from an object toward the center, forming a cone of light. The place where the rays come together is called the *focal point*. A lens forms an image because light comes from different places on an object. Light from above the middle of a lens will bend toward a point below the middle. That is why images are upside down. ▲

A CAMERA LENS FORMS AN UPSIDE DOWN IMAGE

EXHIBIT MAINTENANCE

1. Replace light bulbs as needed.

2. Have spare lenses in lens mounts in the event that one of the lenses is taken. (Tying the lenses to the base with string or chain might seem like a good idea, but it usually means having to untangle the lenses every 20 minutes.) ▲

EXHIBIT▲GUIDE

POLARIZERS

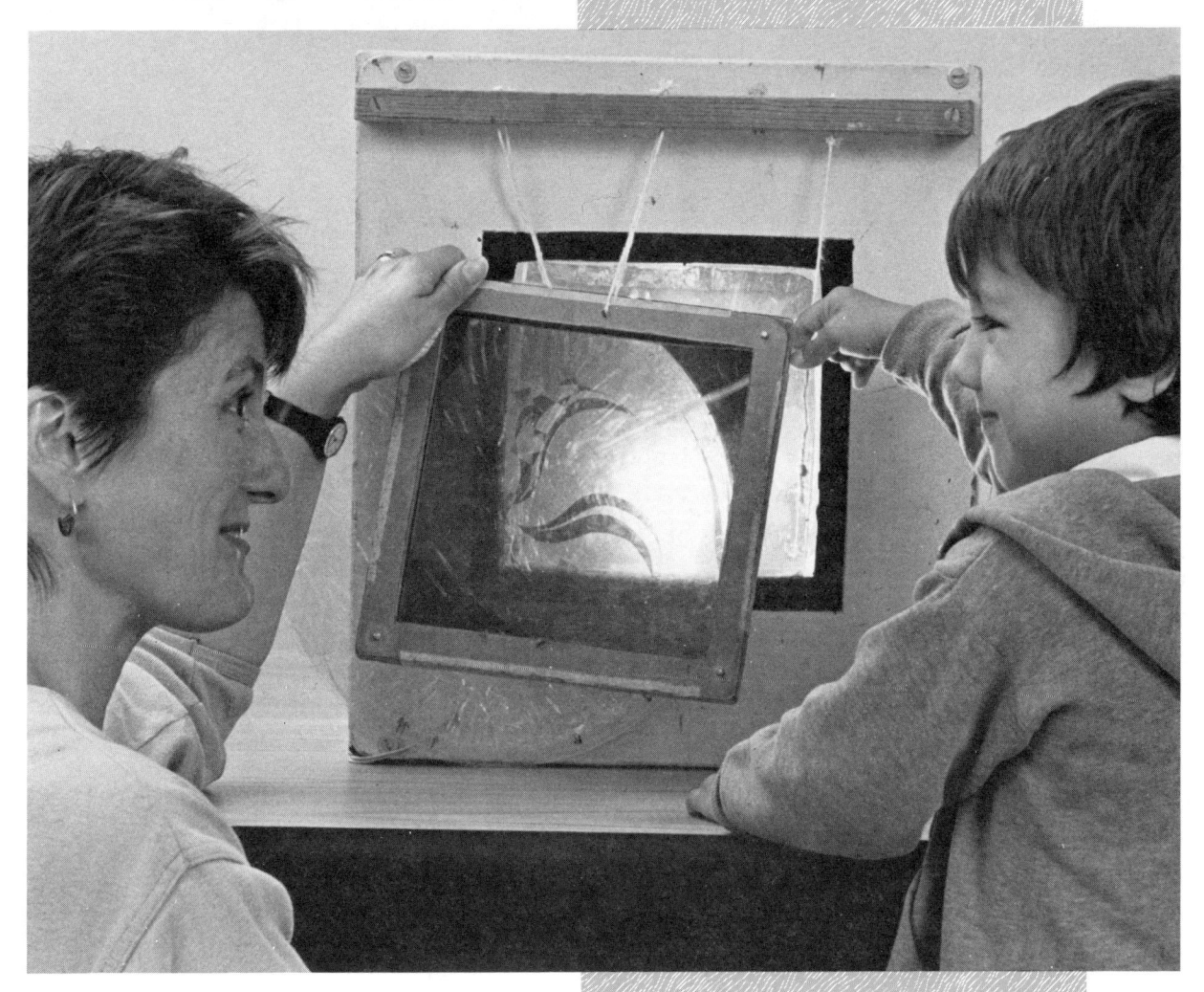

THE WIZARD'S LAB

▶POLARIZERS

Skills
Observing, Analyzing, Finding Patterns

Concepts
Light, Polarization of Light, Color

Themes
Systems & Interactions, Energy, Matter,
Structure, Patterns of Change

INTRODUCTION

Sheets of plastic polarizing material have some amazing properties that visitors can discover in this exhibit. Arrange two polarizing sheets in front of a light source and allow visitors to manipulate various plastic objects in between the two sheets. The visitors will see beautifully-colored changing patterns as they manipulate the materials.

"The Wizard's Words" explain how the polarizing sheets and bits of plastic create the beautiful colors, and how the phenomenon is applied by engineers. ▲

MATERIALS

- 4 clear plastic sheets (⅛" x 12" x 12")
- 1 wood box, at least 12" high x 12" wide x 6" deep
- 1 light bulb with socket, cord, and wall plug
- 1 set of clear plastic utensils: knife, spoon and fork
- 1 roll clear cellophane tape, 2" wide
- 4 heavy strings, 6" long
- scraps of wood and wood screws as needed
- 2 plastic polarizing sheets 12" x 12" (Available through science supply companies such as Edmund Scientific Co. in Barrington, New Jersey.)
- 2 labels

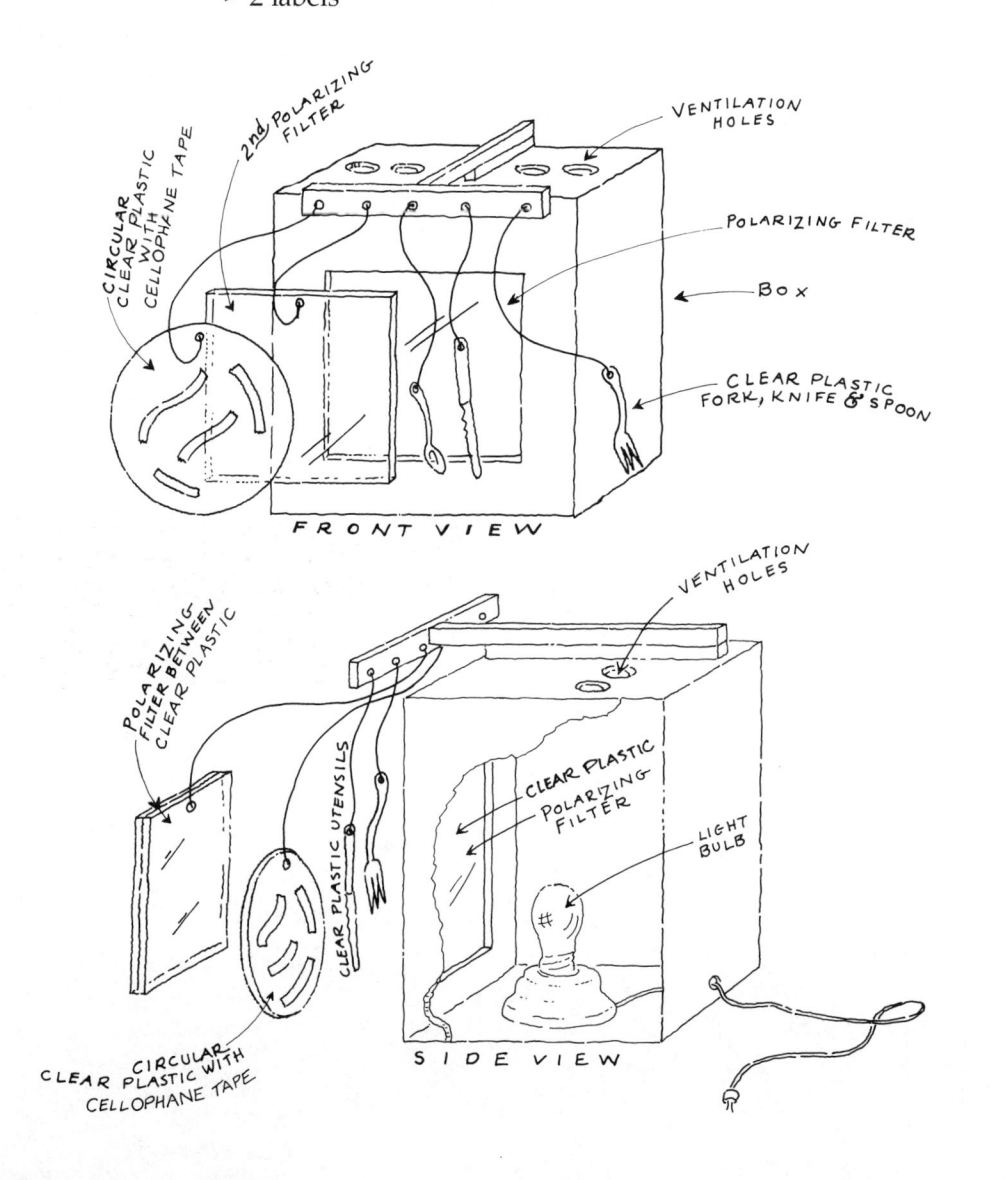

EXHIBIT
CONSTRUCTION

1. Make a wood box 12" x 12" x 6". Leave one of the 12" x 12" faces open to become the front of the box.

2. Mount the light socket, cord, wall plug and bulb in the interior of the box, so the bulb is approximately centered. Drill a few ventilation/cooling holes at the top of the box and on the back, near the bottom.

3. Fasten a 12" x 12" piece of clear plastic over the open face of the box, sandwiching one of the polarizing sheets between the acrylic plastic and the edge of the box. Use screws so the sheet can be removed to replace the bulb.

4. Drill a ⅛" hole in each of the plastic utensils.

5. Create a geometric design of different layers of clear plastic tape on a clear plastic sheet. Drill a ⅛" hole in the corner of the plastic sheet.

6. Sandwich the second polarizing sheet between the remaining pieces of clear plastic and secure by taping along the edges. Drill a ⅛" hole in the corner.

7. Use scrap wood to make a bar near the top front of the box from which to hang the plastic utensils, the tape design, and the second polarizer. Space out the strings as far as possible to avoid tangling. Use string to hang the above items in front of the polarizer box face.

8. Label both polarizing sheets "LIGHT POLARIZER." ▲

The WIZARD'S POLARIZERS

Put pieces of plastic between the two polarizers.

Keep turning the front polarizer sheet. What do you see?

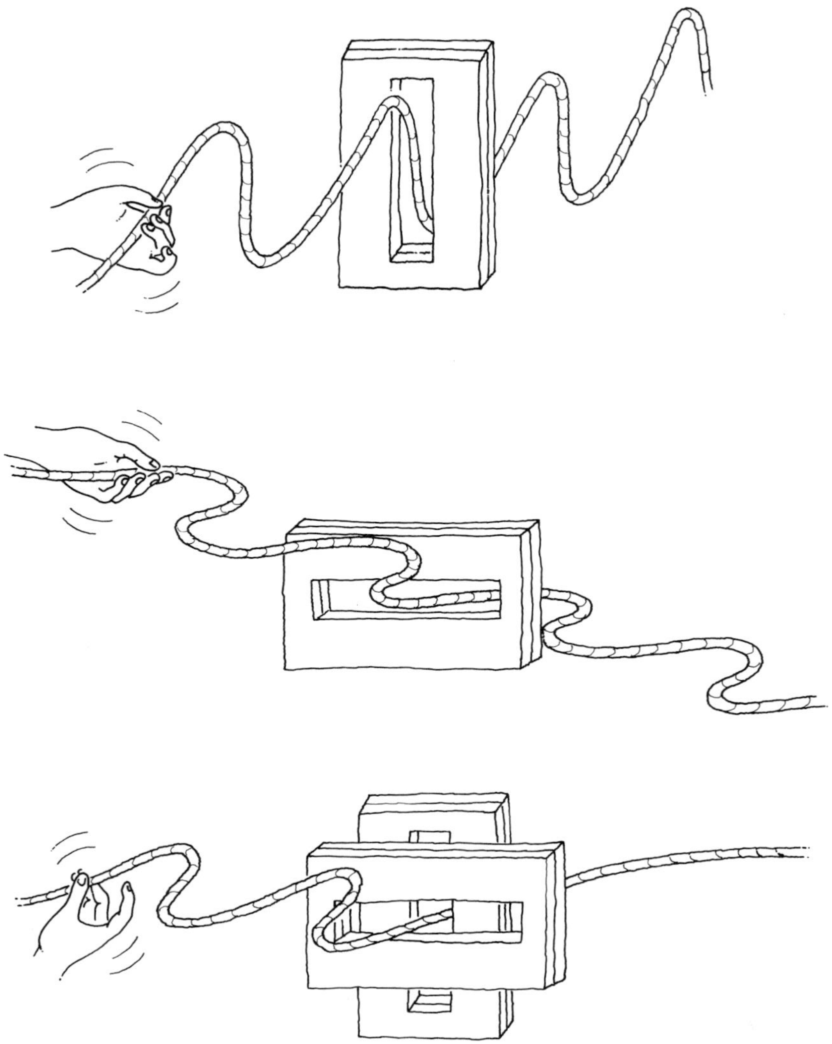

The Wizard's Words About Polarizers

Applications: Pieces of plastic display brilliant colors when placed between two polarizers. Applications of this phenomenon include the following:

▶ Polarizers can be used for quality control in factories that produce thin sheets of plastic to determine if the thickness of the sheets is uniform.

▶ Engineers sometimes build models of bridges or other structures out of plastic and use polarizers to analyze areas where the structure will be under pressure.

▶ Crystallographers use polarizers to see crystal structures that are invisible to the naked eye.

Explanation: Imagine sending waves down a rope by swinging the rope from side to side or moving it up and down. The direction you move determines the *polarization*, or angle of the wave. A *polarizer* for rope waves is a piece of cardboard with a slit. If held vertically, it passes only waves moving up and down. If held horizontally, it passes waves moving sideways. Two polarizers at right angles stop all waves.

Light waves from the bulb are polarized in all directions. Each light polarizer lets through light polarized in only one direction. If the polarizers are held crossways, almost all light is cut out. Now put a plastic object between the polarizers. Colors appear because the plastic changes the direction of polarization. The change depends on the color of light and thickness of the plastic. Thus, light from only certain colors passing through certain parts of the plastic will be polarized at just the right angle, so they pass through both polarizers and into our eyes. ▲

EXHIBIT MAINTENANCE

1. Replace plastic utensils, light bulb, and polarizing sheets as needed.

2. Inspect for damage to wall plug and cord. ▲

EXHIBIT GUIDE

SOUNDS

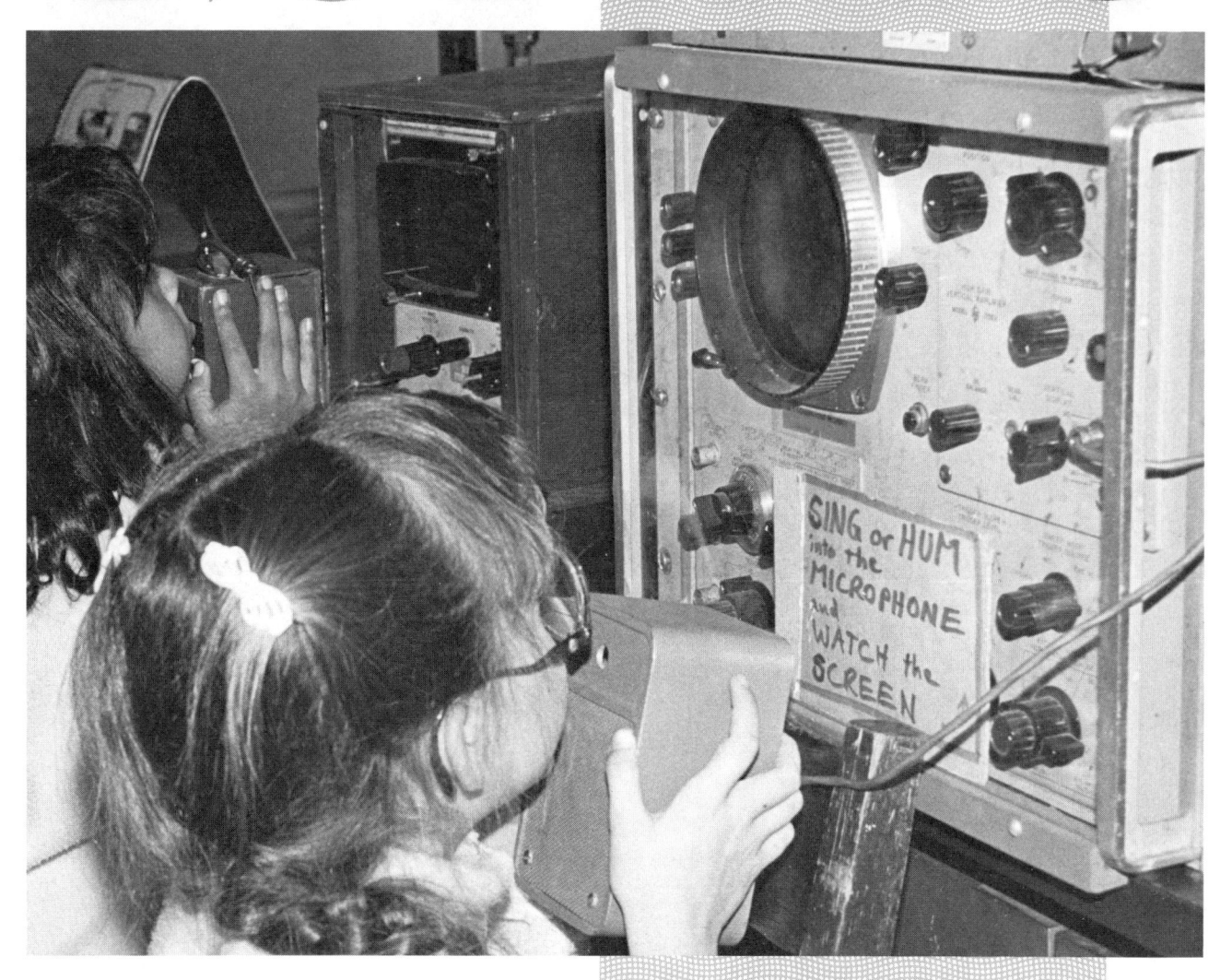

THE WIZARD'S LAB

▶SOUNDS

Skills
Observing, Analyzing, Finding Patterns

Concepts
Sound, Superposition of Waves, Amplitude, Wavelength

Themes
Systems & Interactions, Models & Simulations,
Scale, Structure, Energy

INTRODUCTION

A singer came into the Wizard's Lab and spent about 30 minutes with this pair of exhibits that display sound waves on a screen. Using the first exhibit, *"Seeing" Your Voice,* the singer tested out high notes, low notes, loud and soft notes, every kind of vowel and consonant, you name it! With the second exhibit, called *Adding Sounds,* she systematically explored how two sounds added together as she changed their pitch. While most visitors are not as exhaustive in their use of these exhibits, they find them instructive and enjoyable.

Each exhibit requires specialized electronic equipment, including oscilloscopes, signal generators, speakers, etc. While this equipment is expensive, you may be able to scavenge or borrow the components since they are commonly used in high school physics labs, vocational schools, and electronics repair shops. Some states make surplus electronic equipment available to educational institutions at nominal cost.

If you can only build one of the exhibits, we recommend *"Seeing" Your Voice,* since visitors love to observe the effects of their own voice. The *Adding Sounds* exhibit will be especially interesting if you also have a *Harmonograph* exhibit (as described in this folder) nearby, as the figures it creates are very similar. Visitors can better understand both exhibits by comparing them since the principle of **superposition of wave motion** is common to both. ▲

MATERIALS

"Seeing" Your Voice

- 1 oscilloscope
- 1 microphone or small speaker
- 2 connecting wires, 16 gauge, 18" long
- 1 clear plastic cover to protect the oscilloscope controls

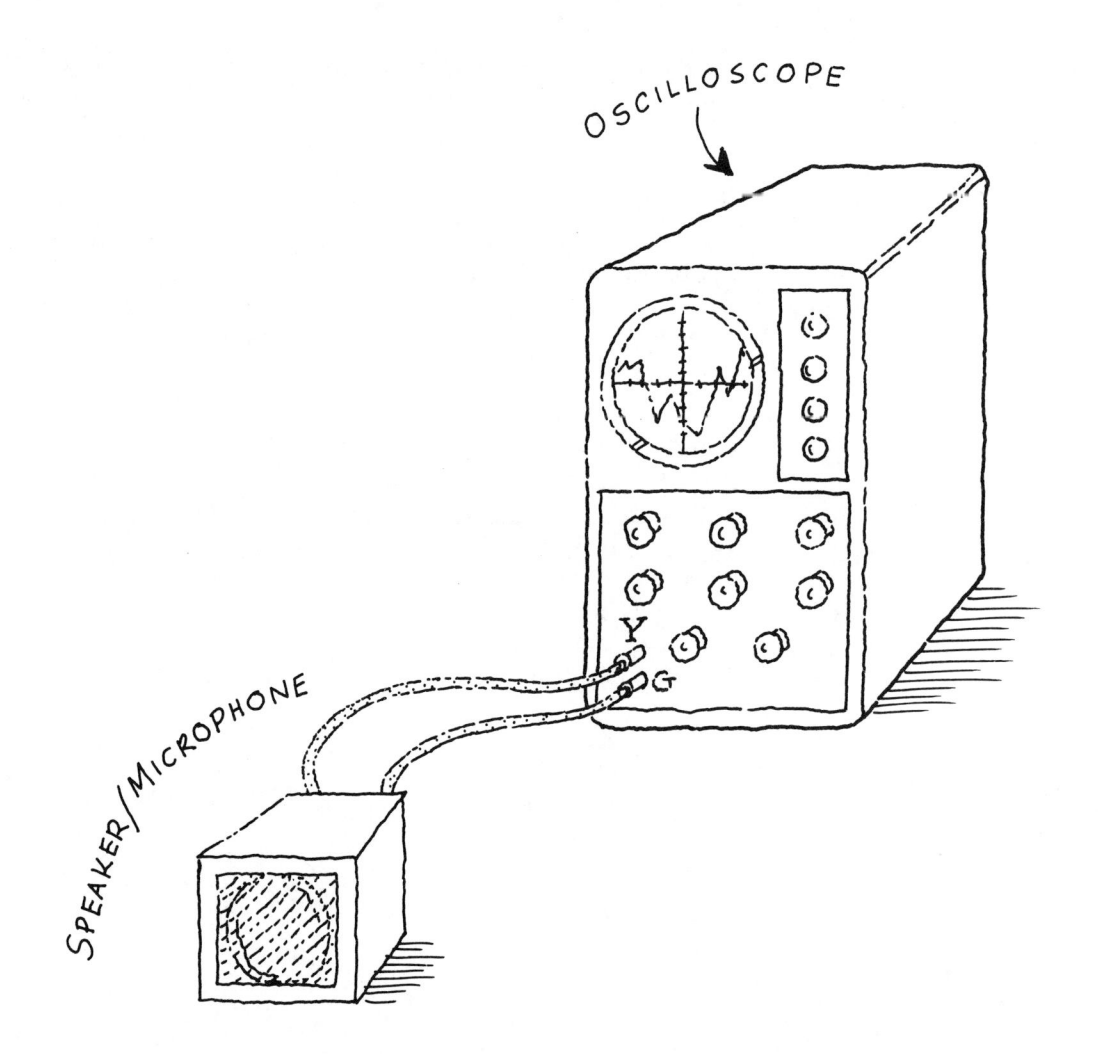

EXHIBIT CONSTRUCTION

"Seeing" Your Voice

1. Connect the microphone to the "Y" input and ground terminals of the oscilloscope. A small speaker can serve as a microphone:

   a. Mount the speaker in a box covered with fabric so visitors do not break the paper cone.

   b. Connect the two wires from the speaker to the "Y" input and ground terminals.

2. Adjust the knobs on the oscilloscope so the sweep line is centered and in focus, the frequency range is in the audio range (50–8000hz), the brightness is near maximum, and y-gain produces waves that are easily observed when you speak in a normal voice near the microphone.

3. Make a removable clear plastic cover for the oscilloscope so visitors cannot touch the knobs, but staff can remove the cover to readjust the knobs when necessary. ▲

MATERIALS

Adding Sounds

- 1 oscilloscope
- 6 connecting wires, 16 gauge, 18" long
- 1 clear plastic cover to protect the oscilloscope controls
- 2 audio signal generators (also called audio oscillators)
- 2 speakers (built-in amplifiers optional)

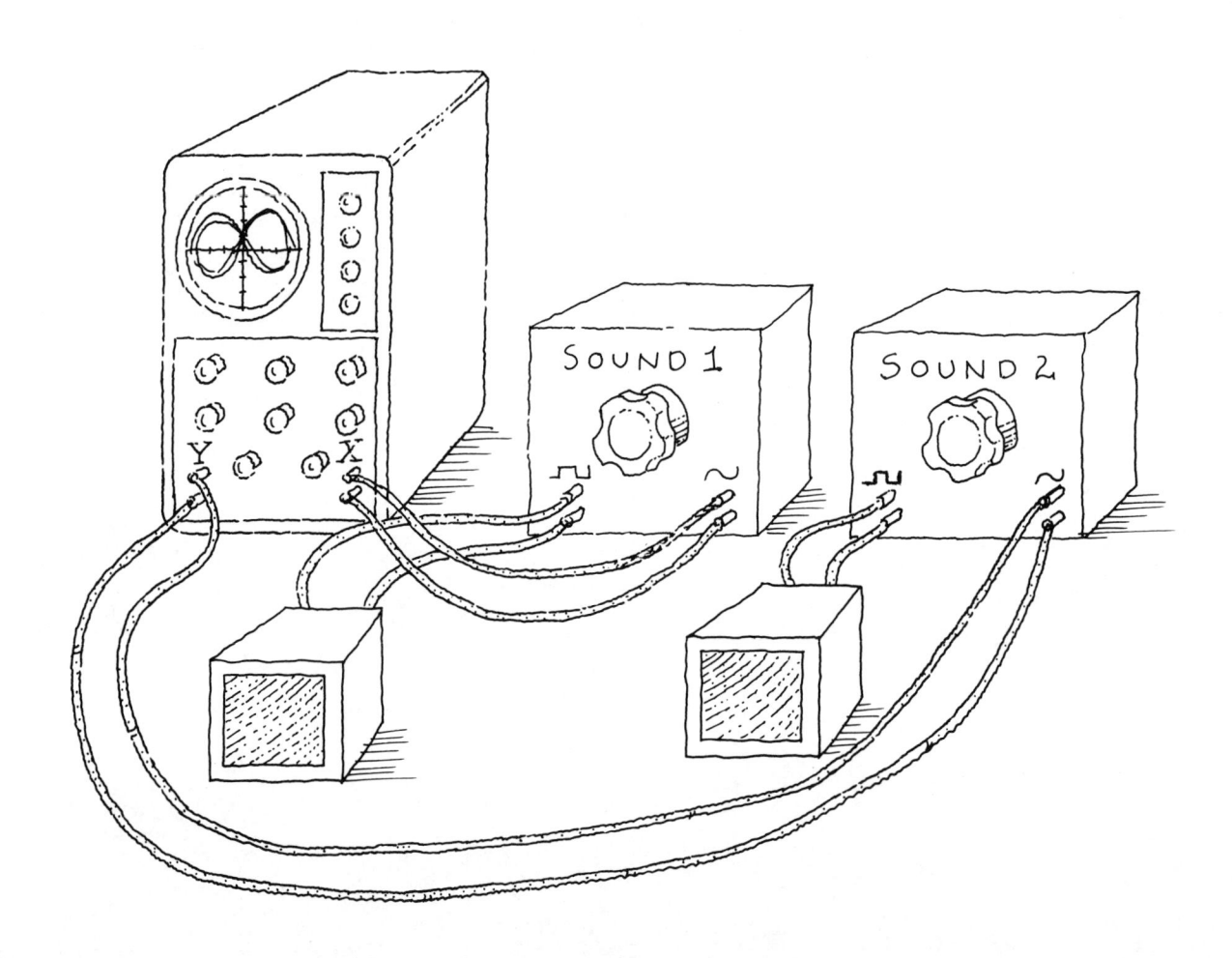

EXHIBIT CONSTRUCTION

Adding Sounds

1. Connect the sine wave output from one audio signal generator to the "Y" input of the oscilloscope, and the sine wave output from the other signal generator to the "X" input of the oscilloscope.

2. Connect the ground terminals of all three instruments.

3. Connect the two wires from each speaker to the output and ground terminals of each audio signal generator. (*Note:* Our signal generator could not drive the speaker and the oscilloscope when both were connected to the sine wave output. However, the speaker worked when connected to a separate square wave output. If your signal generators do not have a square wave output, you can use speakers with built-in amplifiers.)

4. Make a clear plastic cover for each of the audio signal generators that allow visitors to adjust frequency only. Set the other controls so visitors can hear a tone as they turn the pitch knob, from high to low frequency. The amplitude should be low enough to avoid disturbing visitors at other exhibits.

5. If you have a *Harmonograph* exhibit (also described in this folder) place the *Adding Sounds* exhibit nearby. "The Wizard's Words" sheet that explains *Adding Sounds* refers to the *Harmonograph*, so if you do not have one, delete the last paragraph before mounting it near the exhibit. ▲

The WIZARD'S SOUNDS "SEEING" YOUR VOICE

OSCILLOSCOPE

Hum or sing into the microphone and "watch" your voice.

What does a high pitched sound "look" like? A low pitched sound?

Make sounds into this microphone.

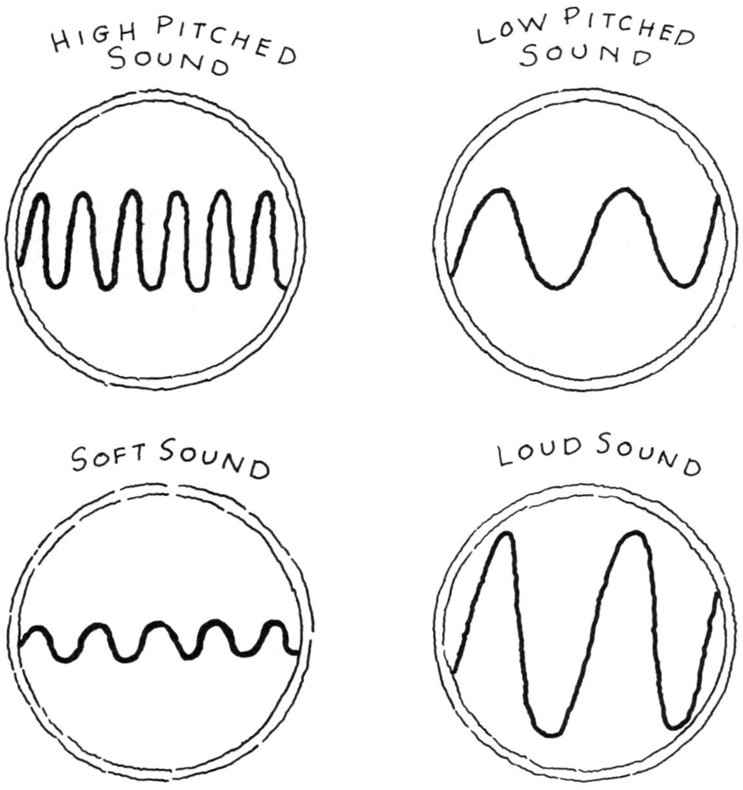

The Wizard's Words About "Seeing" Your Voice

Applications: The machine which makes the sound of your voice visible is called an *oscilloscope*. It is used for many purposes:

- Engineers use oscilloscopes to analyze sounds for improving audio equipment and adjusting the acoustics of concert halls.

- Biologists use oscilloscopes to study the sounds made by different animals.

- Auto mechanics use an oscilloscope to analyze the engine when tuning up a car.

Explanation: When you speak, the voice box in your throat vibrates. These vibrations cause the air to vibrate. In this exhibit you speak into a microphone that turns the vibrations into an electrical signal. The microphone is connected to an oscilloscope that makes the electrical signal visible as a series of waves. The height, or *amplitude*, of the waves indicate how *loud* the sound is, while the spacing between successive waves, called the *wavelength*, indicates the *pitch* of your voice. Try humming or singing high and low pitched sounds and observe how the wavelength changes. Hum louder and softer and observe the change in amplitude. ◂

HIGH PITCHED SOUND

LOW PITCHED SOUND

SOFT SOUND

LOUD SOUND

The Wizard's SOUNDS

What picture do you see when the two sounds are the same pitch?

OSCILLOSCOPE

Make different pictures on the screen by adding two sounds together.

SOUND 1

SPEAKER 1

SOUND 2

SPEAKER 2

Change the sounds by adjusting these knobs.

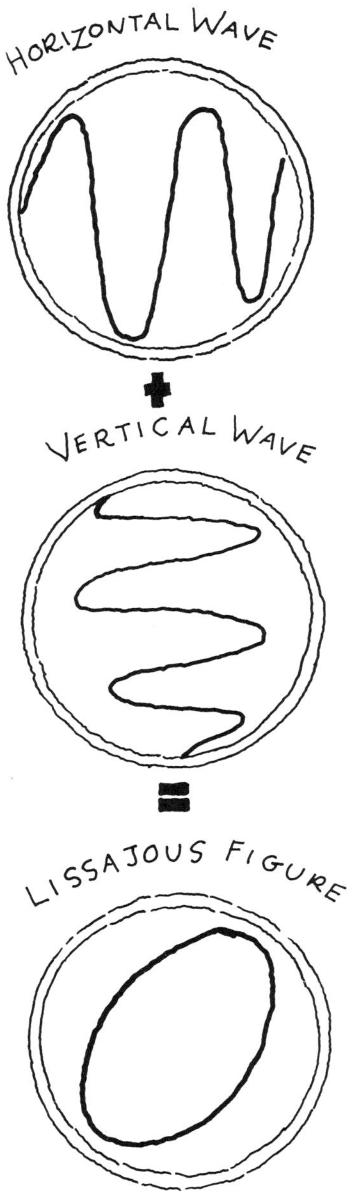

The Wizard's Words About Adding Sounds

Applications: The beautiful patterns on the screen are called *Lissajous figures* after the 19th century scientist who discovered them, Jules Lissajous.

▶ Today, Lissajous figures are used by engineers who need to compare two sounds to see if they are precisely the same pitch (high or low).

▶ Special effects for science fiction movies often include Lissajous figures because they look mysterious.

Explanation: The two boxes with knobs you can adjust are called *audio signal generators*. They each produce a sound. You control the pitch of each sound by turning a knob. The oscilloscope displays these two sounds at the same time, one as a *vertical wave*, the other as a *horizontal wave*. The waves add together to form a more complicated shape called a *Lissajous figure*. Experiment to see how the Lissajous figure changes as you slowly change the pitch of one sound as the other stays constant.

Nearby is a harmonograph that also makes Lissajous figures. In the harmonograph the horizontal and vertical waves are the result of the swinging of a heavy platform. In this exhibit the horizontal and vertical waves result from the addition of two sounds that are converted into electrical signals. The property of many different kinds of waves that allow them to be added together is called *superposition*. ▲

HORIZONTAL WAVE ➕ VERTICAL WAVE ＝ LISSAJOUS FIGURE

EXHIBIT MAINTENANCE

The oscilloscope and audio signal generators may need occasional repair. Other than that, the only thing that can go wrong is an occasional broken wire. Keep spares on hand. ▲

Wizard's Lab Literature Connections

There are many non-fiction works for young people about electricity, magnetism, and other concepts explored in the *Wizard's Lab*. Biographies of scientists, inventors, and mathematicians who contributed to our understanding of these phenomena are also excellent accompaniments to these activities. The first book listed below is a biography, and there are many other excellent ones. Student teams could choose different scientists, read about their research, and report on connections to *Wizard's Lab*. The other books listed below are fictional works, again far from exhaustive, that connect to concepts students explore in *Wizard's Lab*. You or your students may have your own favorite books, and we welcome your ideas!

Coils, Magnets, and Rings: Michael Faraday's World by Nancy Veglahn. Illustrated by Christopher Spollen. Coward, McCann & Geoghegan, New York. 1976. Grades: 5-8.

> Biography of Michael Faraday, discoverer of the electric generator. Captures the spirit of the questioning scientist. Portrays fascinating experiments with electricity and magnets that students can replicate with several of the Wizard's Lab exhibits. Students could try the Wizard's Lab experiments on electricity and magnetism first, then read the book and see if they can determine which ones Michael Faraday is likely to have experimented with or invented.

Chitty Chitty Bang Bang: The Magical Car by Ian Fleming. Illustrated by John Burningham. Random House, New York. 1964. Grades: 4-adult.

> Series of adventures featuring a magical transforming car, an eccentric explorer and inventor, and 8-year-old twins Jeremy and Jemima. Nice combination of technical and scientific information, much of it accurate, with a more mystical sense of how some machines seem to have a mind of their own. A humorous and fantastic literature accompaniment to activities involving technology and inventions.

Danny Dunn and the Swamp Monster by Jay Williams and Raymond Abrashkin. Illustrated by Paul Sagsoorian. McGraw-Hill, New York. 1971. Grades: 4-6.

Danny and friends discover a superconductor which they use in an adventure in Africa involving an electric fish. The explanation of electrical current, resistance and magnetic field on pages 24–26 relates well to *Wizard's Lab*.

Einstein Anderson Lights Up the Sky by Seymour Simon. Illustrated by Fred Winkowski. Viking Press. New York. 1982. Grades: 4-7.

In Chapter 10, "The Spring Festival," the decorating committee gets help from static electricity in placing balloons. (Many other Einstein Anderson books include relevant stories.)

Dear Mr. Henshaw by Beverly Cleary. Morrow, New York. 1983. Grades: 4-6.

A moving story about coping with divorce and being the new boy in school, told through the letters of a 10-year-old boy. In one section, the boy sets out to catch a thief by rigging a battery-powered burglar alarm to his lunchbox, and this invention gains him respect. This section (pages 81-111) could be a literary accompaniment to the activities in *Wizard's Lab*.